I0091476

Broken Branches

A philosophical introduction to the social
reproductions of oppression from an
intersectional feminist perspective

Latashia N. Harris
University of Portland

**Vernon Series in Critical Perspectives
on Social Science**

VERNON PRESS

Copyright © 2017 Vernon Press, an imprint of Vernon Art and Science Inc, on be-half of the author.

All rights reserved. No part of this publication may be reproduced, stored in a retrieval system, or transmitted in any form or by any means, electronic, mechanical, photocopy-ing, recording, or otherwise, without the prior permission of Vernon Art and Science Inc.

www.vernonpress.com

In the Americas:	*In the rest of the world:*
Vernon Press	Vernon Press
1000 N West Street,	C/Sancti Espiritu 17,
Suite 1200, Wilmington,	Malaga, 29006
Delaware 19801	Spain
United States	

Vernon Series in Critical Perspectives on Social Science

Library of Congress Control Number: 2017934976

ISBN: 978-1-62273-088-9

Cover art: Ashley Renee Bey Ex Rel Ashley Harris

Product and company names mentioned in this work are the trademarks of their re-spective owners. While every care has been taken in preparing this work, neither the authors nor Vernon Art and Science Inc. may be held responsible for any loss or damage caused or alleged to be caused directly or indirectly by the information con-tained in it.

Table of Contents

Acknowledgements

To the pedagogy that is born from broken ground.
To our healing, to our restoration, to our transformation.

For Rosie & Ashley

We will always be ART

Introduction

The inspiration for this book stems from the classic song by Billie Holiday, *Strange Fruit*. It became clear to me from the song's simple, blatant and visceral lyrics- that those of us within a United States community context have become complicit and complacent to socially manufactured tragedy. We acquiesce to digesting our social ills as we navigate the oppressive spaces we design. We distract ourselves with the enamoration of arbitrary and manufactured beauty. The egregious dynamics that are at play within our society operate on a continuum and are consistently normalized and accepted.

We witness the battering, the bruising, and the stringing up of bodies hanging from proverbial poplar trees. Do we see that the dynamics of oppression are informed by what we socially plant? Do we realize that oppression is conditioned and not organic? Does our neurocognition assist us in interrupting the inoculation of who we have become? Does our metacognition see beyond our created landscapes and realize what socio-political dynamics exists as by-products on the periphery of our inhabited environments?

Our very being, our value, and our positionality is contingent upon adherence to systemic oppression given birth to from Western hetero-patriarchal white supremacist concepts of power and marginalization. Literature has failed to philosophize more in depth on how or why we as "citizens", intergenerationally become complicit in perpetuating and sustaining the dichotomy of the de jure and de facto definitions and applications of freedom.

The structural belt needed to maintain the status quo of inequity hinges on our complicity *as well as* our approval. From every song of nationalism, every policy seen as a stride towards equality while whitewashing equity, every microinvalidation, every aggression- macro and micro- that exists in the spaces we inhabit, we are faced with the relative truths of our epistemology as well as ontology.

This book was written to challenge the rhetoric of the past, but to also contribute to the emerging narratives of sustainable transformational justice at the convergence of multiple schools of thought. Transformation is the operative term used rather than the word "restorative". Transformative justice recognizes that a system built on exclusion can never be restored to a glory that failed to ever exist beyond propaganda.

When I reference the idea of "strange fruit", there is a paradigm that exists between "black bodies swinging from poplar trees with blood on the root"[1], that we see prevalently today. In my own interpretation as an adolescent, my hope was that the blood of our ancestors dripping on the root, would plant seeds to a new future. A better future. However, the historical precedence of shared power belonging only to hegemonic groups has nurtured a society that would rather carry out abhorrent practices than share power equitably.

This book's use of the phrase "broken branches" refers to how our society is not thriving, but is instead being broken in on an intergenerational level. Broken branches refer to the weight and consequences of maintaining and participating in marginalization and pain. The fruit from our broken branches are the products of our individual and socialized preconceptions being enacted in public as well as private spaces. It is strange to believe that these fruits have flourished, but that... they have. This book seeks to confront those fruits of interaction, induction, indoctrination, policy, practice, institutions, and biopolitics.

Ultimately, the goal if this book is to come to see ourselves as metaphorical arborists, so that the seeds that we plant are cultivated and nurtured with proactive care. No longer can we stand to have our mind's broken –in. Our limbs require justice to thrive. Else, we all shall continue to perish in our humanity, walking the earth, contributing nothing to our vitality and contributing solely to our demise. Inhabiting the earth as the nefarious undead.

This book explores race, gender, sexuality, ability, capitalism, and institutions - specifically education and media. This book seeks to explore and extrapolate upon theory, popular education, intersectional justice lens analysis and the emotional and mental turmoil that is invisibilized within our communities. This book also explores the intra- community conflict that arises when we explore narratives and waves of social justice. This book seeks to ensure that the ways in which we advocate for solidarity don't reproduce and mirror the oppressions by which we have been navigating through all our lives simply because these past dynamics of seeking justice are all we know. This book was written to serve as a push to step further into innovation and work through complex conversations. The analysis that presents itself in the following chapters seek to

---

[1] Holiday, Billie. Strange Fruit

shift away from a narrative that normalizes the accepted benignity of generationally compounded iniquity and inequity. It must also be articulated that every piece of literature has a scope. Therefore, this book cannot nor does it claim to house an exhaustive examination, analysis, or critique on all things plaguing our society or the maladaptive responses to its faults that continue its operation. There's going to be gaps, but that's what expressed limitation and implications for further study and exploration are meant to acknowledge and fill in the future.

Reflective Statement

I am a firm believer in the notion that *nothing* is unbiased. I identify as a queer trans* person of color (QTPOC) assigned female at birth, with invisible disabilities from Montgomery, Alabama. I am a child of a single mother and a child of two parents from rural areas within the State of Alabama. You can't exist there and not pay attention-well I guess you could, but I refused to. I have an M.A. in Urban Affairs from Norfolk State University- a Historically Black College and University, and a B.S. in Interpersonal and Public Communication from Mississippi College, a Southern Baptist Christian College. I have worked in academia as well as non-profit. Through the experiences of my life, I thought it imperative to prepare a manuscript that encompasses the phenomena of the strange fruit and broken branches I've witnessed but rarely seen in literature. I want to explicitly state that, though our lives influence our perspective, these themes do not represent or reflect *just* my experiences, they are not unique. This *could* be considered a piece of "radical" postmodern feminist literature, only if we define the term radical as the amplification of marginalized voices. This manuscript is only radical if we define radical as the presentation of a different narrative juxtaposed to hegemonic ideologies that have colonized the narrative for centuries. Most times it is horribly difficult and usually impossible to *prove* an –ism or a phobia to those that perpetuate them. We tango in feminism, critical race theory, and in society with what claims are legitimate. However, how many narratives or studies must be conducted to "prove" the impacts of oppression and have societal members actively participate in healing these wounds? We find ourselves continuously defending our humanity or trying to live through and prove our disenfranchisement. We understand that those that have to approve or validate our narrative's legitimacy are the hegemonic groups that are not impacted by and commonly perpetuate or benefit from those very oppressions uplifted and brought to the fore of conversations.

  Overall, this book's audience should be everyone. This book is aimed to start or continue conversations from a foundation of intentional explicitness. I hope you enjoy reading it, as much as I enjoyed writing it.

Chapter 1

How We Got Here

What do we mean when we say the phrase "How did we get here?" Whether the question is posed in a time of relative or nuanced joy for some and despair for others, why does the statement come with such ostensible authenticity? There are historical eras preceding our time that we used as our map, model and our guide. In the era of the 21st century, we have seen a surge of racism, heterosexism, xenophobia, white nationalism, ableism, and body shaming run rampant without pause[2]. Notice, I didn't say *resurgence*. There may have been a quell in explicitness socially, but I hold the supposition that the lull of violence does not prove the absence of thoughts to which catalyze, extroverted violence in the first place. Was the lull in comparison to other eras in history due to structural works to minimize and keep wrongdoings out of the public eye, or was it economic prosperity, fear, or actual belief in equality? One thing that can be asserted is that the post 9/11 era created space, from fear and bandwagon effect, to revert to explicitly villainizing all marginalized bodies under the veil of believing that it was for "national security". As this increased villainization rose it resurfaced the resentment, fragility, and insecurity of hegemonic groups. This dynamic made clear how hegemonic groups felt it imperative to retain power, refuse to acknowledge historical indiscretions, and demand that colonial practice be retained[3].

To refer to the aforementioned -isms and phobias as unique to this time is remiss at best. Yet, it *is* a phenomenon that some rhetorical narratives see this era's increased flux of blatant and non-obfuscated discrimination *as* a phenomenon when historical information (present, modified, and/or micro-invalidated or obscured) proves its previous presence and its cycle. It is also bewil-

---

[2] Simpson, George Eaton, and J. Milton Yinger. *Racial and cultural minorities: An analysis of prejudice and discrimination.* Springer Science & Business Media, 2013.

[3] Inglehart, Ronald. *The silent revolution: Changing values and political styles among Western publics.* Princeton University Press, 2015.

dering that some that remain in positions and identities of power have taken the notion of shared and equitable power as an affront to their libertarian perceptions of their achievements. Those in positions of power continuously fail to acknowledge whose access had to be barred so their achievements could come to fruition. Equally troubling is the attempt of hegemonic identities to claim and co-opt "reverse" -isms and phobias[4] to explain how they process the ideas of diversity, equity, inclusion, cultural competency, implicit bias, and justice.

How we got "here" - being space, time, frame of thought, and ways of mental and communicative encoding and decoding- is by societal members instituting Western concepts of power. Western concepts and tactics of power has historically been achievd through violent means, exploitation, as well as lack of equitable distribution of wealth and resources. As marginalized groups have been socialized by their communities to hold a sense of multiple consciousnesses for survival[5], for those in power- a solitary *streamline* of consciousness has been made possible. This difference in consciousnesses is possible because dominant groups hold and control the narrative to which the marginalized have been forced to abide by for limited access within society as opposed to no access at all.

Let it be clear, that one can inhabit privilege and oppression at the same time[6.] However, that highlight should not be used by one inhabiting identities of both oppression and privilege to defend and perpetuate oppression based tactics under the veil of benignity. Nor does inhabiting both privilege and oppression extend the right to pretend one doesn't hold privileges solely because they hold identities that are being oppressed as well. As we continue on with conversations, focused on understanding marginalization and cyclical oppression, it is also necessary to explore the phenomenon of how we recoil at the "-ist" terms (i.e racist or sexist) being a label

---

[4] James, Lois, Stephen M. James, and Bryan J. Vila. "The Reverse Racism Effect." *Criminology & Public Policy* (2016).

[5] Harnois, Catherine E. "Jeopardy, Consciousness, and Multiple Discrimination: Intersecting Inequalities in Contemporary Western Europe." In *Sociological Forum*, vol. 30, no. 4, pp. 971-994. 2015.

[6] Curtin, Nicola, Anna Kende, and Judit Kende. "Navigating multiple identities: The simultaneous influence of advantaged and disadvantaged identities on politicization and activism." *Journal of Social Issues* 72, no. 2 (2016): 264-285.

applied to people, but become inoculated to the very act or perpetuation of -isms (racism , sexism, heterosexism) whether it be covert and/or overt. When we understand that the social repercussions of –isms don't directly impact a hegemonic body in a direct way, but that one's hegemonic silence or participation perpetuates –isms' existence, our critical conversations gain traction that could shift the gears of a dominant narrative.. When issues that limit the livable freedom of a body are discussed, we often see that examples brought to the fore are consistently justified under a rhetoric of normalcy, dismissed, or rapidly explained away with common recitation of rationales given with defensiveness but no critical thought. In contrast, when an abuse of power is cited among those with privilege, the defense becomes a rationale many lay considerable stake in. That rationale being the claim that the marginalized are attacking *their* freedom, by demanding their own[7]. It is as if the dialogue of privilege and oppression is seen as a threat. As if both freedoms cannot exist at the same time. As if ones' freedom must always hinge on the marginalization of another. As if hegemony fears being treated as it has treated others. Under-standing that hegemonic participation is required or expected for interactional dialogue to continue, hegemony often declines to take steps towards engagement in order to protect the freedom it holds as it tramples on others.

I question the rationale that one group's ability to obtain freedom *requires* the participation and overall majority engagement with those that hold identities that benefit from others' oppression. In addition, I question the very real commitment and willingness of the engaged privileged to acquiesce power they did nothing to ob-tain and to dismantle and abdicate a throne whose foundation is positioned on the backs of the oppressed.

The idea of freedom seems to historically and presently rely on bodies most privileged to approve of its use and applicability. This White supremacist heteropatriarchal practice endures from the theft of this land to present day. We continue to ignore, rationalize, and minimize the impact that systemic oppression has had on those who could not benefit from it, that were killed by it, and whose trajectories were limited because of it.

---

[7] Caouette, Julie, and Donald M. Taylor. "Don't blame me for what my an-cestors did." In *Revisiting The Great White North?*, pp. 89-104. Sense Publishers, 2015.

Disenfranchisement, oppression, and -isms are all contingent upon power. Historically marginalized populations that endure oppression have not had the opportunity or the access to the power it would take to deconstruct a system and immediately make it and its institutions work in their favor[8]. This is why prejudices toward hegemonic groups are possible, but oppression or -isms are *not.* Feelings can be hurt- but there is no amount of prejudice that would add to a pre-existing systemic practice that would sway the amount of power someone who holds a dominant identity has or severely debilitate the way of life for someone with multiple hegemonic identities. The systems and institutions of our society work in favor of hegemony. It took over 300 years to perfect the systems of oppression- yet one visible instance of protest has the ability to send people into a rage of anger or fascination. This is not because of the idea of reverse "-isms", it is solely due to the feeling of power (that many fail to accept they have) being threatened and the unwillingness to share power equitably.

Western Imaginary and Imperialism

When the term Western Imaginary is used, it inherently correlates to the ideology that perpetuates the marginalization of populations under the guise of Manifest Destiny, imperialism, as well as Darwinism. The Western Imaginary is a social construct with detrimental implications for those it marginalizes by way of multidimensional immobility. The Western Imaginary dictates the possibility of a prosperous trajectory and the probability of marginalization. The Western Imaginary touts the counterintuitive narrative whereby we rationalize the practices we participate in but also denounce when others practice[9]. Not only does the Western Imaginary impact the way we digest the parameters of ownership through land, it more importantly and directly affects the manners by which our psyche rationalizes marginalization, persecution, and theft with more benign propaganda that allows us to be in the position of the righteous or victorious. Semantics matter. The Western Imaginary can renege on agreements made with surreptitiously motivated goals under the veil of projected aspirations for peace. These peaceful

---

[8] Hodson, Gordon, and Malvina N. Skorska. "Tapping generalized essentialism to predict outgroup prejudices." *British Journal of Social Psychology* 54, no. 2 (2015): 371-382.

[9] Shohat, Ella, and Robert Stam. *Unthinking Eurocentrism: Multiculturalism and the media.* Routledge, 2014.

terms were and are regulated by those in power and ultimately the parameters of these agreements could be reconstituted, redrawn, and the rhetoric can be reconfigured at the whim of those who possess coercively obtained power. We as a collective society are complicit with these shifts. Those in power require our acquiescence culturally, mentally and socio-politically to prevail. Without disruption, the structural oppression pushed forward by those deemed our "forefathers" continues with every true intention they were motivated by under a false egalitarian front.

The Western Imaginary can be exemplified in the colonization of the United States and the disenfranchisement placed on Native populations that inhabited this land before settlement. Upon settlement, there were two proponents of practice that were required for its tactical success; absolution under framed and dehumanizing necessity and participation commonly perpetuated by bystander effect[10].

What is meant by the first requirement- absolution under framed and dehumanizing necessity is evident with clarity in retrospect of the past but can also be identified easily within the present. When society pushes forward a narrative that is contingent on an "us vs. them" framework- one must decide where more power and less precarity lies. There is no *requirement* to choose a side, but neutrality does breed the proliferation of complicity that creates an uneven balance to whatever side has the most momentum. When marginalized groups attempt to use an "us vs them" narrative they are immediately demonized and a critical eye is placed on their bodies as they are scrutinized for not participating in a practice of uniformity. This continual reaction solidifies minoritized groups' inability to gain any form of liberation due to the demand of fascist adherence claiming the title of democracy.[11].

With the notion of absolution under framed and dehumanizing necessity, those with power have consistently absolved themselves from proverbial sins that would otherwise be punished if these tactics were used within their own social group. Keep in mind, I am

---

[10] Mason, Abra S. "Shelby County v. Holder: A Critical Analysis of the Post-Racial Movement's Relationship to Bystander Denial and Its Effect on Perceptions of Ongoing Discrimination in Voting." *Berkeley J. Afr.-Am. L. & Pol'y* 17 (2015): i.

[11] Singh, Jaideep. "A New American Apartheid: Racialized, religious minorities in the post-9/11 era." *Sikh Formations* 9, no. 2 (2013): 115-144.

discussing power from a Westernized framework and not from one where the marginalized *empower* themselves to retain their ability to function within a society that has disenfranchised them through systemic and structural practices. It must also be stated, that when marginalized groups utilize practices of the Western Imaginary, we still add fuel to the automation of our oppression and downfall.

Nevertheless, when groups of power imply that they will be absolved for the destruction of a land or a people and place it under a framework of "cleansing" or necessity due to fabricated precariousness, an interesting thing occurs. The egregious and excruciating actions of genocide and displacement are rationalized so that those in power see themselves as prevailing victims[12]. There is typically a lack of reassessment of the practices suggested due to a bandwagon effect wherein, those who resist are met with treatment that mirrors the treatment of the oppressed[13]. Maybe it is in the phenomenon of the bandwagon effect that we see that fear can coerce one to be complicit, and uplift how the concept of power and privilege can be enticing enough to bring along the willing with feeble rationalizations. The Western Imaginary, imperialism, Manifest Destiny, and Darwinism push many to believe that those who should survive will, and those who do not, were not fit for competition. How can we move to deconstruct this aforementioned assumption when the *a priori* that we *need* to be in competition with one another as creatures capable or rationality, is it's foundation. The problem with rationales is that they don't always have to be rational[14]. When we dehumanize bodies, it's easy to practice disposability. We lose our humanity as we take others' humanity away with the power that we possess. Power in the Western framework demands a process of validation- so who validates it? What we do know is that fear fuels power's validation, but so does relative deprivation, insecurity and greed.

Once the idea of absolution is not questioned by hegemonic parties, the marginalized react in devising methods, strategies, and navigational pathways through their oppression to survive. Though forms of empowerment for the marginalized are projected and

---

[12] Omi, Michael, and Howard Winant. *Racial formation in the United States.* Routledge, 2014.

[13] Furth-Matzkin, Meirav, and Cass R. Sunstein. "Social Influences on Policy Preferences: Conformity and Reactance." (2016).

[14] Simon, Herbert A. "Bounded rationality." In *Utility and probability*, pp. 15-18. Palgrave Macmillan UK, 1990.

taught on an intergenerational level their limitations exist under the auspice of institutions that don't want to see the marginalized thrive. Must the marginalized create their own institutions to escape limitations? And in that theoretical creation of institutions, do we not co-opt the language of our oppressors and continue an authoritarian basis of operation? Would these institutions' mechanism be any different? If so, how so? Is the concept of an institution oppressive in and of itself? Are the ideas of power, privilege and validation catalysts that give life to the practice and actualization of imperialism[15]?

The counterintuitive nature of simultaneous oppression and victimization adopted by those who cause destruction are indeed bewildering. Methods of implementing the ideas of imperialism can be noted from the settlement of the United States to present day gentrification. The goals of these practices are to amass and retain power among the privileged. The goals of imperialistic practice also rationalize direct broken adherence to constitutional documents that were supposed to retain order in a land that was stolen. But when a nation's foundation was created on a baseline of treachery, violence, and deceit- can we really expect those with a settler colonialist mindset to follow their own rules that were only meant to regulate "others" but not necessarily themselves?

This juxtaposed existence of the United States also extends beyond its domestic and drawn ideas of borders. In the era of communism, we see that 1) the definition of communism was explained considerably out of its original frame and 2) the need for global power and manipulation continues regardless of domestic concern under the narrative of peril[16]. Consistently the United States has infiltrated other nations with motives that span from political power to the influence over export and import economic opportunities[17]. Rarely has the United States ceased its imperialistic practices. At times we behave as if we are going to "save" a nation or to be the world's police- but whether it is a genuine decision or not- who asked us to be? It is inevitable that marginalized and vigilant

---

[15] Gines, Kathryn T. "6. Arendt's Violence/Power Distinction and Sartre's Violence/Counter-Violence Distinction: The Phenomenology of Violence in Colonial and Post-Colonial Context." In *Phenomenologies of Violence*, pp. 123-144. Brill, 2013.

[16] Morgenthau, Hans, and Politics Among Nations. "The struggle for power and peace." *Nova York, Alfred Kopf* (1948).

[17] Mohanty, Chandra Talpade. "Under Western eyes: Feminist scholarship and colonial discourses." *Feminist review* 30 (1988): 61-88.

citizens will hold resentment towards a nation that disenfranchises them, but as the United States' encroachment grows upon other sovereign nations, resentment continues to grow beyond United States borders as well. The rose colored lenses the United States is seen from become withdrawn as its oppression is realized to be even more unapologetic and totalitarian on a global context[18].

Within the Western Imaginary, within the global or transnational context, we have seen how not only perpetuated rhetorical frameworks function, but also how continued colonization operates on a larger scale[19]. The United States or its "parent" nation of Great Britain is not the only culprit of imperialist practice. We can see present day how India as well as the Continent of Africa, and the Middle East can attribute some of their disparate dynamics to Western colonized manipulation and infiltration catalyzed by Imperialism and religious overzealousness. The natural resources from these aforementioned lands have been put into the care of capitalistic overseers to ensure the depletion of resources with minimal compensation to the people of that land. This dynamic benefits and funds the proliferation of Western framework oppression based sustainability[20]. The assertion can also be made that the Westernized practice of corruption has been engrained in the aristocracy of these historically colonized lands that European Countries have invaded. The residual impacts of degradation are clear in the minimal quality of life that the depletion of its resources for export has given birth to[21]. Yet and still we find ways to demonize the people of these previously or present day colonized lands for their thought, social, political and economic processes that were informed by Western practices of the past. Western thought evolves in pseudo-inclusivity and socialist efforts, as it fails to understand that there is no ability to know what the uninterrupted trajectory of people of colonialized areas could have been. Because the culture of the colonized was destroyed and replaced with Western concepts that

---

[18] Slaughter, Anne-Marie. "Disaggregated sovereignty: Towards the public accountability of global government networks." *Government and Opposition* 39, no. 2 (2004): 159-190.

[19] Pease, Donald E. *Cultures of United States Imperialism.* Duke University Press, 1993.

[20] Nkrumah, Kwame. "Neo-Colonialism: The Last Stage of Imperialism. 1965." *New York: International* (1966).

[21] Ziltener, Patrick, and Daniel Künzler. "Impacts of Colonialism-A Research Survey." *Journal of World-Systems Research* 19, no. 2 (2013): 290.

required the people's acceptance of the Western framework that assumed their cultural inferiority, it led to automated internalized oppression. These cultures could have already had evolved thought processes that were deleted from history that we can never rediscover, because the Western Imaginary demands only one narrative exists, its own.

The Western Imaginary is so much more than land maps. The Western Imaginary is the forced cultural whitewashing of an indigenous people, it is power and corruptibility, it is the coercive adoption of Western practices with the destruction of previous ways of being so that Westernization in all of its forms becomes the only known way of being. With this erasure of cultures, the tacit operations of democracy and capitalism becomes exposed, but was rarely ever challenged to a degree that could cease its spread, growth or normalized existence. Therefore, we adopt these Westernized ways of existence within a system that will never benefit those marginalized the way that it does for those who benefit from the system's oppression based mechanisms that are vital to its operation. When we discuss how our minds have been colonized, it's clear how we got here. The question is- is there anything we can do about it?

I suppose it is necessary to contemplate, how "power" is achieved within a Westernized framework. Accepted hypocrisy, manipulation, coercion, obfuscation, bribery, violence, and complicity are required components in its infancy and must continue to remain in the fore of a people's mind when they contemplate dissent. The topic of complicity is a delicate one. Historically those who challenge the commonly accepted rhetoric, place themselves in a position where whatever privilege they do have can be wiped away. It is a conditional relationship. For those who are of an oppressed group- challenging the rhetoric can be dangerous in that one's very life is disposable. When a life is lost or dismantled, it's more than just one life- there's a message sent to anybody that it othered, that there are very real and tangible repercussions one will incur if they decide to "defect" from business operating per usual[22]. There is an understandable amount of fear that goes into the complex understanding of how we become complicit.

---

[22] Medina, José. *The epistemology of resistance: Gender and racial oppression, epistemic injustice, and the social imagination.* Oxford University Press, 2012.

The amount of social coercion of the marginalized through manipulation and violence has been prolific. We must consider the cultures that are being and have been taken advantage of through ostensible agreements of peace and partnership[23]. We must also consider the use of firepower in areas where those technologies were not used- and not because these societies did not possess the bandwidth to develop them. We must question Darwinism with the question of: could these cultures have simply found that their societies functioned with prosperity without such technologies? It is reckless to state that disenfranchised people today under Darwinist theory were "conquered" because they were ill equipped or deserving of their humanity less than another race, gender, sexuality, ability, etc. However, when firepower is implemented, and your options are to be killed or have your body taken over- it is indeed a difficult decision, rightfully so, to make and we should take some time to understand the implications of those limited binary options.

We've discussed how complicity can be nuanced, but at times it can be extremely simple. Where the nuance lies within complicity's simplicity is in admittance of the apparent. What is meant when I say "simple" is in that relative deprivation is a part of the human condition[24]. As long as we see someone with something we want, we want more than to just have what they have but to also have more than they possess to make ourselves feel superior. It must also be fleshed out that the simplicity with groups within power is that because of relative deprivation, we fear being put back into a place where we are hyper aware of our relative deprivation. Therein the hegemonic groups rely on being in a position where they are the epitomic figures of aspiration rather than to reside in a position where they aspire to be anything other than themselves. Hegemonic groups understand the power dynamics of our society and in doing so would rather assume positions of power rather than inhabit positions that would require them to find or identify different navigable modes of self-empowerment and efficacy to obtain and practice self-determination as marginalized populations most often

---

[23] Stark, Evan. "Coercive control." *Violence against women: Current theory and practice in domestic abuse, sexual violence and exploitation* (2013): 17-33.

[24] Hogg, Michael A. "Intergroup relations." In *Handbook of social psychology*, pp. 533-561. Springer Netherlands, 2013.

have to do[25]. In short, people like and are obsessed with power that is contingent on a basis of comparison. In the ways we are taught to understand power- to have it, another group has to be oppressed. We have failed to begin the conversation on how we can actually share power or empower ourselves in ways that do not hinge on another group's downfall.

When I discuss the simplistic housing of complicity, what I mean is that people socialized within a Westernized world, want power. The question continues to be - at what cost? It becomes clearer as we continue with the same practices of disposability- that there may be no lengths when we look at the wars, infiltrations, murders, and delineation of who is subordinate. The costs paid and lengths taken perpetuate the persistent subjugation of a people[26]. In what could be minimized to the smallest practice of marginalization that extends one's power, the seed has already been planted in our psyches of rationalizing and making all pathways to obtaining that power acceptable, no matter how theoretically unacceptable.

Furthermore, the question of what incentivizes participation in oppression or in digressing from the colonized framework of complicity is also called to question. Can it be for the greater good? Who defines what the greater good is and can there be common ground on what its definition is? Does one require an incentive to do the "right" thing beyond humanism under the theoretical framework of inclusive and intersectional feminism? Figuring out what pushes complicity is where difficulties lie in facilitating its discussion.

Do we ultimately need an incentive or are we capable, despite our socialization, to push for equity even if it requires us giving up power to actualize what that type of freedom could look like?

In conclusion, the Western Imaginary is delusional. It pushes ideas of freedom, without extending that opportunity to everyone. It pushes the idea of democracy when the marginalized are not counted or proportionally represented. We push the idea of sovereignty without respecting it with other nations or with Native populations. We push the narrative of how others are oppressing a

---

[25] Leake, David, and James Skouge. "Introduction to the special issue: "Self-determination" as a social construct: Cross-cultural considerations." *Review of Disability Studies: An International Journal* 8, no. 1 (2014).

[26] Giroux, Henry A. *Twilight of the Social: Resurgent Politics in an Age of Disposability.* Routledge, 2015.

people, as we continue to do so ourselves. We demand adherence to policies when we bend and break them at our whim. We discuss and sing about life, liberty, and the pursuit of happiness when we know it's not applicable to bodies that are being controlled by the perpetuated practices of the Western Imaginary. We discuss libertarian practices as if everyone has been extended the same opportunities to achieve a livable and dignified life[27]. We convince ourselves of things we know not to be true. Here in lies the nuanced simplicity. Can we admit that we don't practice what we preach collectively? There fails to be alignment in practice and rhetoric. Does the Western Imaginary demand we fortify its construction? There are more questions than answers. If we want to ensure we don't fall into a Polybian cycle of anarchy to achieve a new "dream" that can be inclusively actualized, we must continuously question our social theories, applications, and ontologies. The American dream is a myth to the dispossessed.

Ownership

When we delve deeper into understanding the concept of ownership, the Western Imaginary rationalizes the most arbitrary of practices into legitimacy. Western European countries have colonized land despite those who were existing there before them with the ill seated rationalization of dehumanization and contextual worthiness[28]. It is inconceivable as to how we make the Western Imaginary real and attempt to hoard land and legitimize a practice that illegitimately places claim on a land and a people. Who extends power to crystalize this practice? Colonization displaces people, coercively seizes not only lands but ways of life, cultures, bodies, minds and made their previous existences unrecognizable under the guise of Western ideologies. We talk about ownership, but not about theft. We talk about belonging, but not about encroachment. We talk about the democratic importance of collective voices when under dominant narratives, few bodies are heard and silencing of the marginalized is paradoxically ubiquitous. When the United States discusses ownership, the rationalization of colonialism is one drenched in the rhetoric of doing what we have to do to protect

---

[27] Cotter, Anne-Marie Mooney. *Culture clash: an international legal perspective on ethnic discrimination.* Routledge, 2016.

[28] Pels, Peter. "The anthropology of colonialism: culture, history, and the emergence of western governmentality." *Annual Review of Anthropology*(1997): 163-183.

"our people". But whose people are those? It is most certainly not all those that inhabit the land. The psuedo- inclusionary approach of having representatives that share no common experience or empathy of the marginalized to act in the best interest of the marginalized people is an affront. Moreover, these representatives, represent without actually understanding that their very function under this rationale within a systemically unjust system is marginalizing in and of itself. We expect bodies to abide in tandem with this Western rhetoric of ownership, not benefit from it, and be owned by its very practice[29]. Why is it that we have not continuously questioned the protection of this idea of ownership that has been placed upon us through the implementation of the Western Imaginary? Representation without competence or experience in unique forms of marginalization can only at best function in a representative capacity with a semi-permeable consciousness.

The sense of ownership is one engrained in the psyche of privilged American traditionalism. But when many are met with this commentary, the conversation typically derails into a narrative of allegiance or dissent under the previously mentioned "us vs. them" narrative. This happens despite what's conventionally considered to be "right", and what's irrefutably *true* with limited attention given to dehumanization, idealized absolution, and abhorrent practices necessary for owenership to exist as we commonly understand it.

When we discuss ownership, we don't discuss it from a perspective of origination that falls outside the parameters of propaganda based on the Western Imaginary. This non-inclusivity of holistic perspectives of all those impacted gives way to only one side of a story being told[30]. It is understood that varying and transgressive narratives may be subjective. But when all narratives aren't included, that invalidation in the dominant narrative drives the way that a culture is received, recited, and fuels the way a culture and society is engineered to practice exclusion. The idea of ownership's origination is not one that is solely harbored in conventional archetypes of historical data. It is important to know that the stories of cultures have been desecrated by the very imaginary that staked

---

[29] Furnivall, John Sydenham. *Colonial policy and practice.* Cambridge University Press, 2014.

[30] Young, Robert. *White mythologies: Writing history and the West.* Psychology Press, 2004.

claims on the narrative of history and its intergenerational dissemenation. This imaginary is inducted into the cannon of our common core beliefs and understanding. The byproducts of biopolitics gain traction with intentional invalidation of other vantage points. These vantage points are invalidated to heighten the productivity of manufactured patriotism and creates socially acceptable consequences for failing to adhere to patriotism's exlusionary constructed principles.

Power Marginalization, and Capital (Economic):
Social, Governmental, and Economic Systems

The idea of power engrains itself in nearly every aspect of our lives under the rule of the Western Standard. Power is simply an entity or a method that continues to hold possibility. What is pivotal to understand, is how you gain power and what you decide to do with it. Power can be used for neutralization, perceived good or conceptualized evil. Often those living within a Western framework exchange definitions with these words as contexts suits their pursuits[31]. The United States has used power along with its "citizens" to rationalize behavior in a Darwinist understanding of competition[32]. We have glorified our endeavors while villainizing others' for utilizing their autonomy abroad and domestically. Our collective nation nevertheless fails to collectivize or include variant voices that stray away from the intent of those that rule over our society, its policies, and its institutions[33] in a hegemonic fashion.

As mentioned before, we rarely attempt to personify what shared power could look like. We have never tried to create a model of power distribution that could wean ourselves away from the "us vs. them" rhetoric. Often, power can be seen as definitively "good" or "bad", but what we must seek to examine is who dictates the definition of "good" or "bad". Power has been understood within a Westernized framework. The fruit we bear from the social seeds planted perpetuate the rhetoric of absolution under falsely categorized good intentions and imperialism. Imperialism is a malignancy.

[31] Rodriguez, N. "Emptying the content of whiteness." *White reign: Deploying whiteness in America* (1998): 31-62.

[32] Ham, Ken, A. Charles Ware, and Todd A. Hillard. *Darwin's Plantation: Evolution's Racist Roots*. Master Books, 2007.

[33] Parry, Benita. "Problems in current theories of colonial discourse." *Oxford Literary Review* 9, no. 1 (1987): 27-58.

Imperialism must be called out and deconstructed so that its practice can stop being blended into normalization. We practice power based imperialism on each other interpersonally, and it is entrenched within the system by which we willfully answer to. Power is used for mental molding and in practice upon each other on a people to people level. At some point we have to figure out, in what ways we can use power to ameliorate the destruction it has had the ability to cause when exercised to disenfranchise. We marginalize based on our complicity to the concepts and dynamics of power we cling to.

The concept of power is not real but we breathe life into it by agreeing to its validity and adhering to its contextually prescribed applicability. However, much like many constructs- power does have real implications that endure throughout multiple eras in similar or mirroring ways. Society gives power to the definitions and the acceptability of pathways that gain and accept power in exchanges. Power is its own form of currency. Power also knows its exchange rate varies from body to body based on the constructs of social "markers". Without that complicity or shared agreement of those varying exchange rates, the definitions of acceptable power retention or gathering would hold no weight.

When we explore power, we fail to consistently talk about the distinction between power and self-empowerment of the marginalized. Throughout history we have seen that when those that have been oppressed by widely accepted practices and uses of power attempt to empower themselves, they are met with the common consequence of punitive repression. Society continuously falls short of calling out this dysfunction. In this failure, we fail ourselves and make any thought of equity or equality an ideology we never truly wanted to see come to fruition.

Power cannot be discussed without pinpointing the ways in which it operates systemically with forms of government as well as economic systems. It is easy to give the nation state exceptions to its use and abuse of power. Innovation in methods that created shifting power structure alternatives is a difficult conversation and rarely one many find the bandwidth for. How the economic system is constituted is intrinsically interconnected to our form of government. The capitalistic system that we abide by, abuses it power. This abuse is evident when we dig deeper in the ways that we ignore treaties, agreements, and policies without pause for economic gain under neoliberal Manifest Destiny techniques[34]. Our economic approaches of dereliction are also evident in the way we hold transactional relationships with other nations. We use these relationships to deplete other nations' resources and infringe on their political, economic, and social sovereignty. This infringement is acted upon to achieve our gross domestic product goals by benefitting from the ways these nations export and import their goods[35]. Often, we economically and covertly support global governments when it's in our best interest. Our fight *for* a particular government is not democratic at all nor is our intervention truly or solely about human rights. Our interventions are commonly about commerce that favors the economic interests of the United States[36]. Economy is much like our forms of government; it never exists or operates as its definition claims. Our economy and governmental processes posits itself to be one glorified thing in theory and ambiguously deceitful in practice. Therein, the question of: can government or economics exist in a way that mirrors its practice with its theory? And if not, why do we not call it by the names that its practice embodies instead of conceptualizing terms in ways that are not applicable to the pure definition of such used words?

Coerced Collective Narrative- Paradigms and Implication under the Guise of Americanism Tactic

Earlier, we discussed how pushing for a widely accepted narrative among those in positions of power and the marginalized create face precarity when transgressing from the acceptance of a coerced narrative. Throughout time post the flapper era- the United States has tried to strike fear into the body of its inhabitants to collectively agree on a narrative that demanded nothing less than compliance and uniformity[37]. In essence, the narrative was not agreed to by the proletariat but adherence was demanded from them by the privileged. We have placed expectations on the people of this nation to be familiar with songs of nationalistic pride even when its words

---

[34] Zoysa, Richard de. "America's foreign policy: Manifest Destiny or Great Satan?." *Contemporary Politics* 11, no. 2-3 (2005): 133-156.

[35] Smith, Karen E., and Margot Light. *Ethics and foreign policy.* Cambridge University Press, 2001.

[36] Skocpol, Theda, Peter Evans, and Dietrich Rueschemeyer. "Bringing the state back in." *Cambridge* (1999).

[37] Parker, Alison Marie. *Purifying America: Women, cultural reform, and pro-censorship activism, 1873-1933.* University of Illinois Press, 1997.

exist in complete contradiction to the practice of the environment by which its marginalized inhabitants live within. Despite realities, there is an expectation to behave as if the words in the Constitution and a Declaration of Independence were applicable to everyone. The acceptance of these aforementioned documents, their inconsistency of applicable rights, and the overlooked incongruence between those in power and those subjected to its power ignores the practices of settler colonialism. This dynamic proves that marginalized populations have been placed in a position where compliance is expected despite the prohibitive political and economic measures taken to prevent access to liberty.[38]

It is evident that post-World War II, the United States has made several attempts to surveil and monitor those who are seen as dissenters. This can be gleaned from the propaganda placed within our visual and audiological reach through media[39]. The Committee on Un-American activities pushed the United States into a new era where freedom of speech and thought was criminalized, despite constitutional articulation of rights[40]. The Red Scare and Pink Scare of McCarthyism[41], the Berkeley protests[42], and the anti-Vietnam war effort[43] are prime examples of how freedom is fleeting when it goes against the grain of accepted narratives. Freedom of assembly and freedom of speech are acceptable as long as they operate on a paradigm of the current narrative of the United States. As long as narratives perpetuate an "us vs. them" narrative and way of thinking. The narraive of an "us" is bound by those that hold the most power to dictate the direction that the defined "us" is going in. Our colonized minds do not take notice of this unfree-freedom. We

---

[38] Omi, Michael, and Howard Winant. *Racial formation in the United States.* Routledge, 2014.

[39] Kellner, Douglas. *Media culture: Cultural studies, identity and politics between the modern and the post-modern.* Routledge, 2003.

[40] Fisher, Linda E. "Guilt by expressive association: Political profiling, surveillance and the privacy of groups." *Ariz. L. Rev.* 46 (2004): 621.

[41] Heale, Michael J. *McCarthy's Americans: red scare politics in state and nation, 1935-1965.* University of Georgia Press, 1998.

[42] Mitchell, Don. "The liberalization of free speech: Or, how protest in public space is silenced." *Spaces of Contention: Spatialities and Social Movements* (2016): 47.

[43] Moore, Kelly. "Political protest and institutional change: The anti-Vietnam War movement and American science." *How social movements matter* (1999): 97-118.

continue to operate in a way that implicitly and insidiously professes that the juxtaposition does not exist or rationalize an explanation for a situations' contextual exception to staple mores that dissolve our freedoms. When we discuss coerciveness and complicities, our narrative is pivotal for this discussion. We often behave as if the narrative we hold is collective, as if there is a national stance. The leverage held against marginalized bodies or those with privilege and power are placed in a position that shows how close they can come to being stripped of whatever humanity they have. This conditional freedom is contingent on, at the very least, ostensible alignment to governmental and social expectations of allegiance and decorum. Without this collective narrative the nation-state fails to "control" its people. Without control and compliance, the Western Imaginary fears the loosening of centralized power in what purports itself to be to be a democratic society.

The Idea of Democracy: Aristocratic Oligarchies

The way we treat democracy within the United States resembles its basic definition[44] in minuscule practice only. What we commonly hear is that existing as democratic republic implements equitable checks and balances. From the Electoral College to the way that our Congress is structured internally, it's very clear that centralized power is its intention. When decisions lay within one body - how can they speak for their people from a solitary vote? The issue with democracy is that if we are following a collective and nuanced voice- how can every voice having a vote determine anything other than the reifying of majority vs. minority practice. These practices continue to disenfranchise those that are in marginalized and minoritized groups or positions. What is difficult about democracy is that we don't implement the notion of equity in our governmental infrastructure properly. We focus more on equality and fail to create mechanisms that create pathways to liberation. We acknowledge the historical pretext of oppression, but without disruption and reconstructing our governmental and economic infrastructures, we allow the automation of oppression to continue under another name. Conversely, the democratic practice could extend popular vote representation on every issue, but it again could

---

[44] Schlozman, Kay Lehman, Sidney Verba, and Henry E. Brady. *The unheavenly chorus: Unequal political voice and the broken promise of American democracy.* Princeton University Press, 2012.

disenfranchise those that have historically had no power. Democratic processes can also allow representatives, if chosen, to decide for a conglomerate of people. These decision making powers are given but representatives' individual biases are not taken into account. We also can't be sure if representative's ultimate goal of getting reelected isn't at the fore of their minds as motivation as opposed to the issues that they cast votes on[45]. Within democracy or a democratic republic, the welfare of the entire society is rarely taken into account. Democracatic representation and dynamics are contingent on individual wants, needs and, relative deprivation.

What we truly live in is an aristocratic-oligarchic representative democracy. Those that hold the highest percentage of wealth hold the most power in our country, not the people. Regardless of what perceptions its positions teeter over to, we must revisit how those who possess power and privilege typically vote in their best interests despite the notion of possible shared and equitable power. We rationalize our oppression within our votes. This leaves the question of what system is possible. Is democracy even at its purest form, viable for uplifting the marginalized or centering the most impacted? Or are we as inhabitants of this land, subjected to the colonization of the mind that proliferates and continues the disenfranchisement of groups of people in a systematic way? The questions always lie within what the alternative could be. We should push ourselves away from defunct models to determine what works for this society as it exists and how the future of our society could exist under alternate structures as the best form of itself. When we discuss the form of democracy that we live in, we fail to question its process. We have also failed to determine in what ways our system of checks and balances are substantiated and evaluate its functionality with intentions of change. There is also something to say about the notion of pervasive authority over our lives. Do we as human beings require that authority to behave humanely and equitably? Who decides the definition of humane and the parameters and scope of equity? And do we become complicit in participating in a system fueled by oppression with the mere hope that it can be transformed? Can you transform something by working from its old parts and its co-opted framework? If as Audre Lorde stated, "the

---

[45] Dewey, John, and Melvin L. Rogers. *The public and its problems: An essay in political inquiry*. Penn State Press, 2012.

master's tools can never dismantle the master's house" [46], then is there only futility in trying to "fix" systems in place? Are we inherently required in processes of transformation (rather than restoration) to walk away from all that would and should be dismantled?

Epistemology

When we discuss how we got to where we are now, we have to discuss epistemology. The things we know. The things we know are under the strain of what has been taken away and what all groups have not been given access to in understanding their history. We fail to have the ability to empower people through their own historical narrative because it is something that has been erased , devalued, and rewritten for many. For example, African Americans that have a lineage that was coercively migrated had their family structure dictated and controlled. Their languages and their faith were beaten out of them, and their psyche were manipulated (although double consciousness did persevere in some dimension). This was done so that African Americans would function as controlled people within a society that was structured and defined by those who destroyed their history. Without knowledge of one's past, there is a tremendous amount of power and hope that is lost. When we force languages, faith, cultural mores, and ways of life to be purged from a people and allow them limited access to the systems to which they were placed in, their collective social mobility is significantly improbable.

We think that policies that push for diversity, inclusion, equality, or equity can "fix" centuries of oppression in less than fifty years. Those who don't embody these marginalizations fail to understand the type of impact historical marginalization has had on a people.

Native communities were victims of genocide[47], Africans and African Americans were subjugated to slavery and "post-colonial" era practices of marginalization that maintained power dynamics[48]. Asian communities were interned , exploited in labor, and excluded

---

[46] Bailey, Alison. "Strategic ignorance." *Race and epistemologies of ignorance*(2007): 77-94.

[47] Churchill, Ward. "Indians are us? Culture and genocide in Native North America." (1994).

[48] Ng, Wendy. "Japanese American Internment." *The Wiley Blackwell Encyclopedia of Race, Ethnicity, and Nationalism* (2016).

from immigration[49]. Asian communities are now expected to abide by the principles of a model minority myth while still not reaping any privileged benefits as they are constantly invisibilized[50], Middle Eastern bodies are seen in negative archetypes that impact the level of safety held in daily life[51] as they are met with terrorist oriented supsicions. Latinx communities have been targeted as perpetrators of soiling the American labor force[52] and American way of life through villianization. Women and trans or non-binary marginalized genders have been infantilized, hypersexualized, and demonized[53]. When we discuss compounded marginalized identities, the societal negative impacts become more intense and harrowing. This societal and governmentally approved behavior and perceptions of dismissal and disposability have informed these stereotypes and stigmas. Stereotype and stigmas fuel the cycle of the social becoming structural, and the structural informing the dynamics of acceptability of insidious thought processes and actions. It is a difficult thing to rebuild from that within a society that still deems your mere as existence as deviant. It is difficult to survive in an environment that stereotypes your body at every turn based on the invalid rhetoric of the past. Those that perpetuate marginalization and devaluation interestingly find some way to co-opt and appropriate the culture created[54] . These cultures cultivated by marginalized populations despite oppressive practices. However, when these cultures are expressed by marginalized bodies they are devalued. When cultures are appropriated, society assigns higher value to appropriative bodies of privilege. This higher value assignment further glorifies colonial theft. Hegemonic groups continue to claim the cultures of those they oppress as their own

---

[49] Lowe, Lisa. Immigrant acts: on Asian American cultural politics. Duke University Press, 1996.

[50] Lee, Stacy J. Unraveling the" model minority" stereotype: Listening to Asian American youth. Teachers College Press, 2015.

[51] Awad, Germine H. "The impact of acculturation and religious identification on perceived discrimination for Arab/Middle Eastern Americans." Cultural Diversity and Ethnic Minority Psychology 16, no. 1 (2010): 59.

[52] Reimers, Cordelia W. "Labor market discrimination against Hispanic and black men." The review of economics and statistics (1983): 570-579

[53] Oswin, Natalie. "Critical geographies and the uses of sexuality: deconstructing queer space." Progress in Human Geography 32, no. 1 (2008): 89-103.

[54] Freire, Paulo, and Donaldo Macedo. "A dialogue: Culture, language, and race." *Harvard Educational Review* 65, no. 3 (1995): 377-403.

under a collective narrative without apology. Women were and are seen as less than. They are seen as "belonging" to male identities with no acknowledgment of their self-agency[55]. Non-heterosexual populations were and are seen as deviants.Those with varying abilities were considered bodies who should not be visible. The implications of the way we see bodies directly impacts policies, practices, and acceptable social behavior that otherwise would be deemed as lamentable on white heterosexual able-bodied males. Our minds have become inoculated to the practice of injustice. We make minimal space to discuss the impacts of the epistemology of ignorance and what that does to generations and generations of human beings. Society at large reduces arguments of this trauma to "whining"[56] because this is not a problem that impacts hegemony, so the conversation is not valued.

The epistemology of ignorance impacts marginalized groups within the realm of biopolitics regarding race, gender, sexuality, or ability. The guiding recognition of humanity within the Western framework is the construction and power given to whiteness[57]. From this foundation, body value is scaffolded based on what other marginalization one holds in respect to access. The ability to survive is ingrained in the ontology of the marginalized. However, we must expand on that ontology in frameworks that also allow us to thrive despite what was taken away.

Define American

It is understood that many a people cross imaginary borders that seek to dictate where and when bodies can move through them. It is also understood that people come to the United States seeking to achieve whatever they autonomously choose to seek. We cannot, however, use migratory patterns as a variable in evaluating the overall quality of our nation with a concluded rating of flawlessness. Living or wanting to live here does not mean we cannot critique this country. People living or wanting to live here does not mean we get

---

[55] Collins, Patricia Hill. "It's all in the family: Intersections of gender, race, and nation." *Hypatia* 13, no. 3 (1998): 62-82.

[56] Ferber, Abby L. "The culture of privilege: Color-blindness, postfeminism, and christonormativity." *Journal of Social Issues* 68, no. 1 (2012): 63-77.

[57] Tascón, Sonia, and Jim Ife. "Human Rights and Critical Whiteness: Whose Humanity?." *International Journal of Human Rights* 12, no. 3 (2008): 307-327.

to ignore our systemic breakdowns. What we can critique, is how we treat the notion of immigration overall. One may choose to come to the United States due to asylum or by simple attraction. However, we view entry into these borders with a savior complex to glorify our self- importance or use immigration as a place of barter. The dilution of your culture and the adoption of the historical oppression based mental colonization, for your citizenship[58]. We rarely have the emotional capacity to discuss the mourning that we go through when we realize that our assimilation or acculturation does not grant us full citizenship as an American. That full citizenship is this a term given de facto to privileged white bodies. Epistemologies are taken away, destroyed, or released in hopes of being seen as a full person. But it is clear through those afore-mentioned processes that if you have to give up parts of your heritage to be seen as a full person, then this is not a melting pot. It is an American nightmare rather than any dream that has been advertised through propaganda. This is not to say that people bow down to this subjugation at all times. If one has the ability to be subversive enough- another adopted stream of consciousness can be created and developed for survival while returning to the inter-nal core of who you are. If you want entry in this nation, the United States implies that one must assimilate to the dominant narrative, colonialism (and one's subjugation to it) and expectations at the border[59] You can't critique. You can't have critical explicit ques-tions. You have to prove your queerness in ways stereotypically applied to queer bodies[60]. Some who attempt to migrate are also tasked with navigating sexual assault[61]. The constant threat of being

---

[58] Ainslie, Ricardo C. "Cultural mourning, immigration, and engagement: Vignettes from the Mexican experience." *The New Immigrant in Ameri-can Society: Interdisciplinary Perspectives on the New Immigration* 355 (2014).

[59] Alba, Richard, and Victor Nee. *Remaking the American mainstream: Assi-milation and contemporary immigration.* Harvard University Press, 2009.

[60] Luibhéid, Eithne, and Lionel Cantú Jr. *Queer migrations: Sexuality, US citizenship, and border crossings.* U of Minnesota Press, 2005.

[61] Ticktin, Miriam. "Sexual violence as the language of border control: where French feminist and anti-immigrant rhetoric meet." *Signs: Journal of Women in Culture and Society* 33, no. 4 (2008): 863-889.

deported[62] and detained and becoming criminalized[63] are issues
that many immigrants are faced with when their identities are devalued in the United States context. They inherit historical oppression
that is applied to minoritized bodies, despite different epistemologies and histories. Many immigrants come to this nation with hope
only to be hit with the undeniable truth that they have been placed
in a new ranking system paradigmatically aligned to colonial concepts of body value and prescribed degrees of entitlement to mobility. We have racialized the term immigration[64] . We have conflated harm, terrorism[65], economic fear, and the fear of scarcity[66]
with brown and black skin and any other marginalized intersections
that are present in a body. When critical conversation is had about
migration and a sense of belonging, we begin to see just how precarious actual citizenship is and who exactly holds the keys to one's
citizenship. Through resistance, we take these keys back as a signifier of our demand for freedom, our humanity and our rightful
citizenship beyond borders and of the world. Therefore, is critique
of our nation directly correlated or equated to what is un-
American? In the land of the "free"? If yay say the readers then I
counter with – what is American beyond colonization, conditional
socio-political citizenship, death, theft, fabrication and de facto
indoctrination?

Defining the term patriot seems to be closely related to unwavering and unconditional acceptance. I'm not sure if we get to choose
to be a "patriot" in that sense, but we know we were told to be,

---

[62] Arbona, Consuelo, Norma Olvera, Nestor Rodriguez, Jacqueline Hagan, Adriana Linares, and Margit Wiesner. "Acculturative stress among do-cumented and undocumented Latino immigrants in the United States." *Hispanic Journal of Behavioral Sciences* 32, no. 3 (2010): 362-384.

[63] Kalhan, Anil. "Rethinking immigration detention." *Colum. L. Rev. Sidebar* 110 (2010): 42.

[64] Cobas, José A., Jorge Duany, and Joe R. Feagin. *How the United States racializes Latinos: White hegemony and its consequences.* Routledge, 2015.

[65] Saeed, Amir. "Media, racism and Islamophobia: The representation of Islam and Muslims in the media." *Sociology Compass* 1, no. 2 (2007): 443-462.

[66] Matheis, Christian. "US American Border Crossings: Immigrants, Poverty and Suzanne Pharr's' Myth of Scarcity'." *Philosophy in the Contempo-raryWorld* 18, no. 2 (2011): 47-59.

without question. We know we are told to continuously fight for a nation that fights for a few and not all those who live within this country. I am aware, however, that the term patriotism gets used as leverage for our compliance due to the fickleness of our citizenship. And I am aware that we hide the history of our worldly destruction through subterfuge and manufactured narrative in ways that guide and control our behavior, speech, and semiotics of our social and political environments.

Confronted

When met with the seemingly daunting confrontation of acknowledging privilege and complicity in oppression, we often see the fragility[67] of those who embody hegemonic identities. Fragility surfaces the defensiveness of the privileged as they invalidate and delegitimize the lived experience of the marginalized. These behaviors are exercised with the power the privileged most often claim to not hold. In other instances of fragility, we bear witness to the reduction of structural systemic issues into a personal or interpersonal anecdotal problem. It's easier to digest personal problems rather than be confronted with structural ones and determine where one's complicity lies. The centering of the hegemonic population's processing through their guilt[68] takes over the narrative, ignores the impacted marginalization parties, and colonizes space. This practice attempts to overshadow the voices directly impacted from the very marginalization being discussed. This often occurs within spaces that initially sought to deconstruct and move forward, with accountability, the colonization of space and bodies. We witness another peculiar byproduct of decolonization based dialogues when those who embody hegemonic identities equate the articulated impact of groups being marginalized, as a enlistment to a culture of self-victimization[69]. This cognitive distancing tactic of invalidating experiences again reduces societal issues down into being interpreted as solely personal rather than a structural struggle as well. Reduction and dismissive minimization evades critical

---

[67] DiAngelo, Robin. "White fragility." *The International Journal of Critical Pedagogy* 3, no. 3 (2011).

[68] Steele, Shelby. "White guilt." *The American Scholar* 59, no. 4 (1990): 497-506.

[69] Mahoney, Martha R. "Victimization or oppression? Women's lives, violence, and agency." *The public nature of private violence: The discovery of domestic abuse* (1994): 59-92.

thought. This practice's goal is to distance privileged groups from any complicity to and any liability or responsibility in collaborative oppression. This distancing comes from a rhetorical foundation of libertarianism and a distorted conceptualization of personal accountability without context and overall hasty generalization[70]. Negative hasty generalizations by those who do not hold marginalized identities seek to find a rational explanation of –isms and phobias they don't encounter that make them feel comfortable. This approach is often taken to avoid discussing the blatant structural oppressions present on any level of social interactions and dynamics constructively. These generalizations are made to vilify marginalized groups as the products of their failures. These rationalizations want to believe that the work of policies have created a better life for all citizens. Because the marginalized don't have visible chains (save for prisons) on their wrists, neck, and feet, *everyone* is believed to have a chance now. Because the presence of residual impacts of oppression and continued implicit practices of oppression remain, we cannot define the lack of visible shackles to be a signifier of progress. We didn't fix centuries of death and destruction with less than 50 years of policy. Hegemonic groups may wish to cognitively distance themselves and claim they don't see race, gender, sexuality, or ability- but our systems and institutions (and those who administratively work within them) certainly do. Because our systems see and have historcally created minoritizing policies, it is absurd to claim that we as society don't allow that dynamic to persist when it benefits us. The very statement that alludes to not acknowledging a marginalized identity has an intention of togetherness. However, the statement exudes the privilege to opt out of acknowledging or celebrating difference and it opts out of acknowledging unique residual historical impacts.

We don't want to deal with someone else's truth, a demographic's story, or the common denominators of oppression that surface an undeniable trend. We don't want to get messy, even if it's a mess we allowed to perpetuate. We don't want to talk about it, so we say the injustices expressed aren't not real. Privileged bodies and systems use power and influence to redefine the image of the marginalized to appear to be self-pitying, dramatic, hysterical, and irrational. This practice isn't new, it mirrors the ways in which women who wanted to speak their own minds were treated before they were

[70] Neblo, Michael A. "Three-fifths a racist: A typology for analyzing public opinion about race." *Political Behavior* 31, no. 1 (2009): 31-51.

commonly institutionalized[71] as a tactic of control. Therefore, the continued pacification and delegitimizing of lived realities cyclically prevails. We've been socialized – those with privilege and oppression. We find ourselves arguing over who gets to be "right", who gets to remove responsibility and practice erasure or distancing, and who gets to have a dignified life. The magnitude of importance for dignified life is not comparative to any other pairing. Making it clear that the power to control lives should never be up for consideration, and the inalienable right to have the ability to live a dignified life should never have to be fought for. No one should have to prove they deserve to live, simply because of the identities they hold.

The nature of victimization is an interesting one, but moreover I see the culture of victimization represented largely by hegemonic groups[72]. Victim status is used to, as stated previously in the text, validate the use of oppression *or* to distract attention from the narrative of the marginalized. This distraction is used so one can prove that they are a "good person" or a "humanitarian". Humanitarians don't ignore voices. Humanitarians don't silence voices with their power by saying "we're all human beings" without understanding the very real implication of social constructs. Humanitarians don't get to behave as if residual impacts of explicit oppression didn't create implicit oppression and choose to ignore its presence. Humanitarians don't rationalize marginalization or its impacts and humanitarians don't get to be part-time when it's convenient. Humanitarians don't listen to someone say "I am dying" and then ask "what did you do" in return. Humanitarians don't get to not ask themselves what are they an accomplice to that's hurting people. Humanitarians don't get to back down when it's time to do the work in daily life as opposed to a short conversation about allyship. A humanitarian doesn't get to call themselves an ally and not advocate in the ways that the impacted express they need. For that matter, self-proclaimed feminists don't get to do that either. Walk away from the co-opted terms if you're not going to do the work, because it is *a lot* of work. Some in marginalized communities however, have walked away from the terms already. They have walked away

---

[71] Lerner, Harriet E. "Early origins of envy and devaluation of women: Implications for sex role stereotypes." *Bulletin of the Menninger Clinic* 38, no. 6 (1974): 538.

[72] Dixon, Travis L., and Daniel Linz. "Race and the misrepresentation of victimization on local television news." *Communication Research* 27, no. 5 (2000): 547-573.

because they saw that inclusion and solidarity simply was not coming to fruition. The ways that humanism and feminism ostensibly
defined itself did not show itself in practice or in response to inclusive and intersectional critique.

Overall, the historically marginalized *are* victims and survivors of
systemic and institutional exclusion, but we build grit[73], resilience[74], and self-efficacy regardless. That self-efficacy and expectation to maintain it, however, does not assist in healing the trauma
that our exclusionary society fails to interrupt[75]. That efficacy, too,
does not at all negate the oppression still present within our society.
The information being surfaced about the impacts of marginalization are not new. We can't continue to placate to the idea that marginalized voices are invalid when they critique. The themes and
strings of nooses and chains present in the lives of the marginalized
are in the words of the most impacted. The marginalized have oper-
ated on multiple streams of consciousness intergenerationally for a
significant amount of time as a survival tool. This tool taught has
not secured safety. These consciousnesses are now converging as
impacted communities decolonize their being. They are expressing
how they navigate in a system and within institutions that never
developed the infrastructure for them to succeed. The frame is breaking and new seeds are being planted in our minds. We as a societal
community will experience growing pains but these social moments
aren't occurring suddenly. They've been a long time coming.

Neuroplasticity

This initiated conversation on "how we got here" creates pathways
to discuss the way that tactics have been used to colonize land and
also minds. Within the same vein of discussing the broken branches
that fail to grow because of models of oppression, we must explore

[73] Duckworth, Angela Lee, and Patrick D. Quinn. "Development and validation of the Short Grit Scale (GRIT–S)." *Journal of personality assessment*
91, no. 2 (2009): 166-174.

[74] Wexler, Lisa Marin, Gloria DiFluvio, and Tracey K. Burke. "Resilience and
marginalized youth: Making a case for personal and collective meaning-making as part of resilience research in public health." *Social
science & medicine* 69, no. 4 (2009): 565-570.

[75] Harvey, Mary R. "Towards an ecological understanding of resilience in
trauma survivors: Implications for theory, research, and practice."
Journal of Aggression, Maltreatment & Trauma 14, no. 1-2 (2007): 9-32.

whether a new foundation of understanding is possible. Is it possible to move forward with a future in true acknowledgement of our past. This is where the discussion of neuroplasticity enters. Can we shake our generational socializations and our planes of paradoxical consciousness that fuel oppression. Can we shift our mental framework in the spaces that we inhabit? Do we feel that our restructuring would appear as "weakness" to others nations? Does it matter? Can our ontological praxis reconfigure itself by using the plasticity of our mind frames? The concept of neuroplasticity suggests that this mental shift is plausible[76]. However, there is no way of predicting how much effort it would require to enact or sustain mental shifts. There isn't enough information available to indicate what it would take to broaden the scope of social reconfiguration in thought, action, and construction in regards to the disruption of othering and self-awareness. The hope is that our neurological sensors are not static, that our psyche is malleable enough to become dynamic and flexible. After 300 years- can we deconstruct and unpack our Western epistemologies and create another way of knowing and understanding bodies that can affect our society in a positive structural way?

Again, more questions than answers- but this text was always meant to start conversations rather than assume itself robust enough to give direct, overarching and all fitting answers to anyone.

---

[76] Ivey, Allen E., and Carlos P. Zalaquett. "In the Special Issue on Social Justice Leadership." *Journal for Social Action in Counseling and Psychology*3, no. 1 (2011): 102.

Chapter 2

Whose Body Matters?
Biopolitics & Criminalization

The commentary following social media visibility of marginalization, brought into prominence via hashtags, has created a conversation concerning whose life matters to a diverse and wide audience[77]. On the most fundamental level, all lives *should* matter but
the way our society operates, it is irresponsible to reduce the conversation down to the theoretical, knowing we don't reside within a
utopia. The statement that "all lives matter" is only a distraction
and it digresses from highlighting the importance of lives that continue to be marginalized. Privileged bodies have never been invisible, erased, or devalued. Critical attention given to the urgency of
the continued dehumanization of marginalized bodies should not
feel like a threat or juxtaposition to altruistic humanism. We center
emotions of privileged guilt or anger, and the fear of the privileged
in losing power, more than we give needed attention to rectifying
the structural damages that have nearly decimated a marginalized
people.

For example, when pitting Blue Lives Matter vs. Black Lives Matter against one another- there's no need to fall back on an "us vs.
them" narrative. It is true that life is something that should be re-
vered- but different bodies with various identities have been shown
repeatedly through structural, systemic, organizational, interpersonal and individual dynamics that by de facto operation- all lives
do not matter to the same degree. In the instance of blue lives mattering and discussing the police force- those who enter into the
profession recognize the precariousness of the occupation they
chose. Those that were born with black and brown hues of melanin
should not have to experience precarity because of their skin color.
Yet and still, skin tone continues to be a societal hazard or a crime.

---

[77] Freelon, Deen Goodwin, Charlton D. McIlwain, and Meredith D. Clark.
"Beyond the hashtags:# Ferguson,# Blacklivesmatter, and the online
struggle for offline justice." *Available at SSRN* (2016).

That reality is not a comparison that should recklessly be constructed to prove a point wherein a chosen occupation is pitted against the criminalization of a body upon birth. The authoritarian socialization of our society is obsessed with power being legitimized over another body. The symbolic capital used by police forces and bodies that have the power to sanction state sponsored violence have created a culture whereby violence is glorified depending on what "side" you're on. Systemic structures of power are made of people who are too inoculated by violence and power to resist the adoption of white supremacist and heteropatriarchal perceptions and practices. The difference between those in control of systemic structures and citizens who are not, is that their nation state affiliated behavior is systemically protected and rationalized. We live in a society where the demands of compliance are uninterrupted when presented by bodies of authority with little room to discuss nuance. The dominant narrative concerning the valuation of bodies informs perceptions and preconceived notions in a monolithic vacuum. The valuation comparison of bodies' conversation redirects attention to the privileged and is an implicit justification of the violence placed on marginalized bodies and fuels stigmas attached to them. When we stray away from understanding the precarity of the occupation- this is not to say there is no appreciation for the positions that they have taken. But we cannot leave it unspoken that the institution of the criminal justice system is fraught with historical injustice that cannot be easily ameliorated. The way the criminal justice system functions in its clandestine, unjust, and marginalizing operations is the problem. The bodies who are complicit in that unjust operation irrefutably perpetuate structural oppression.

There is a distinction when we say Black Lives Matter or that Native lives are continuously oppressed with minimal visibility, that sexual assault survivors are never "asking for it", that other words can be used to express perspective without hurting someone with varying abilities. However, each distinction calls for the understanding of experiences and intersectional analysis to create a foundation of responsible and inclusive social justice practices. Concerning sexual minorities, it has been made abundantly clear that they too have gone through cycles of criminalization as well as considerable violence. Those with varying abilities are continuously micro invalidated from our collective United States narrative[78]. We fail or refuse to recognize the ways we treat and value the narratives and the lives of the marginalized. The reason there is no uplifting of privileged lives mattering is because society has always made it abundantly clear through socialization and corrupt practices that their lives have always mattered. We should be able to have productive conversations regarding whose life matters, whose doesn't, why that is so, and what can be done by now, but it seems that we still struggle.

When we say that Black Lives Matter, that Native lives are present and that their rights of sovereignty, safe water, land and treaty protections are being pilfered, it's because the dominant narrative seemed to have forgot. When we say that women's bodies should be ensured safety and respect, that sexual minorities are human and not deviants, it is because their value is continuously depleted and society says nothing. When we say that those with varying abilities are fit to be included in our community, deserve access, and demand to know why we would ever think otherwise- we are calling out our society and demanding they recognize the ills it has caused. The fact that we must articulate whose body matters as a reminder indicates the inoculation of the masses. This inoculation shows that society also refuses to see that the marginalized are not now, nor have they ever been "safe".

So yes, fundamentally all our lives matter- but let us not pretend that we as a society have not placed body values on particular identities. Marginalized voices seeking justice are constantly met with combative force and we often employ the aid of those within the criminal justice system to perpetuate oppression rather than disrupt it.

Body Caste Systems; Body Value; Body Control (Socio-Politically)

How is it that we deem darker skin, female identified bodies, Lesbian Gay Bisexual Transgender Queer Questioning Intersex Asexual Two Spirit (LGBTQQIA2S+), and those with varying disabilities less than socially. We devalue and then implement policies to make a definitive statement of their othering. We use superficial de jure efforts of concern and inclusion as a tool to seem progressive

---

[78] Mogul, Joey L., Andrea J. Ritchie, and Kay Whitlock. *Queer (in) justice: The criminalization of LGBT people in the United States.* Vol. 5. Beacon Press, 2011.

enough. These efforts are made without extending any full access to a different social, political or economic sphere. Anything that would create social mobility is constantly not accessible and creates a caste system. These de facto caste systems prove themselves difficult to navigate even as amendments to our constitution were made. The social detriment of caste systems are equally, if not harder, to backpedal on than actual policies. It is society who was complicit in bringing these caste systems to fruition[79]. This was done so with generational socialization, policies, accepted behavior - among other tools. What is a phenomenon is that as socialization takes hold and policies are accepted, we follow these guides even if we know they are counterintuitive to who and what we claim ourselves to be. We automate our irrational rationalizations but we don't put that much energy into unpacking our unwavering allegiance.

Not only have there been practices of enslavement and "justified" genocide[80], the argument deepens when pseudo-science is brought into the conversation that discusses inferiority on a fundamental basis. These things we are exposed to that retain power with the privileged are and have proven nearly impossible to wash away. We ask now are there still de jure or de facto caste systems, and the answer remains clear that there are[81]. We have found ways to circumvent policies by proliferating the degradation of a people in other formats be it in post slavery Jim Crow laws[82], segregation[83], scientific inferiority rhetoric[84], or criminalization and institutionalism in subpar mental health facilities[85].

---

[79] Dumont, Louis. *Homo hierarchicus: The caste system and its implications.* University of Chicago Press, 1980.

[80] Power, Samantha. *"A problem from hell": America and the age of genocide.* Basic Books, 2013.

[81] Siegel, Reva B. "Constitutional Culture, Social Movement Conflict and Constitutional Change: The Case of the De Facto Era. 2005-06 Brennan Center Symposium Lecture." *California law review* 94, no. 5 (2006): 1323-1419.

[82] Woodward, Comer Vann. *The strange career of Jim Crow.* Oxford University Press, USA, 1955.

[83] Omi, Michael, and Howard Winant. *Racial formation in the United States.* Routledge, 2014.

[84] Haller, John S. *Outcasts from evolution: Scientific attitudes of racial inferiority, 1859-1900.* SIU Press, 1971.

[85] Corrigan, Patrick, Fred E. Markowitz, Amy Watson, David Rowan, and Mary Ann Kubiak. "An attribution model of public discrimination towards persons with mental illness." *Journal of health and Social Behavior* (2003): 162-179.

These circumventions are and were rarely challenged. One of the most horrific and abhorrent being the criminal justice system that continues to disproportionately house racial minorities at an outstanding rate[86]. Again, the economic oligarchy comes into play in our representative democracy. This oligarchy favors those who want to profit from the criminalization of bodies of color and could care less for them as a people. Marginalization compounds in documentation, sexuality, gender, and ability. When we realize that the governmental systems we live in are not the ones we learned of we are faced with options to resist or become compliant despite disenfranchisement. At what degree of consciousness to this juxtaposition do we become complicit in our own oppression? How would we break free or walk away from it without falling into the criminal justice system? Is falling into the criminal justice system fundamentally any different from the imprisonment of de facto marginalization? It is worth saying that we do have power to define our own freedom without complying to things that go against the grain of our values, but this is never without consequence. The power given to a system may very well outweigh the power you take back for yourself. However, the weight of power is debatable when we are met with the option of freedom of the body. We must also explore the tolerance level of oppression as it stands alongside the access and opportunity that we do have. At what point are those access points in sustenance or mobility simply not worth the tolerance of oppression. Is any authority that guides the way we exist in space defined as oppression? If we define oppression as what exists but we endure it, are we not perpetuating it ourselves? When we realize that the systems to which we abide by are broken, do we participate in these broken systems with hopes of itself regulating and fixing itself? Or is this an expenditure of energy and false hope without active participation in dismantling the inequitable processes by which it runs? Are we willing to walk away from the things that we have to build a new infrastructure of something that could work or do we keep participating or accepting the presence of governmental mechanisms that are focused on our capitulation rather than our liberation? And when, exactly, is the breaking point for us to say yes or no? Is conditional acceptance of a system's dynamics with options for amendment and edit possible as it has been in the past in a substantive way? When can we get to a point

---

[86] Hudson, Barbara, and Barbara Hudson, eds. *Race, crime and justice*. Aldershot: Dartmouth, 1996.

where we are willing to rebuild from rubble, based on Polybius, there will always be rubble to clean up through processes of governmental restructuring. Who will be present and aid in transformation and who will be against "order"? Anarchy may be an ideology of a few to disrupt what isn't working, what serves to control us. However, after the system is broken down, can anarchist ideology shift to help sustain a community that functions in the ways that we wish it to? If we should not recognize authority that seeks to destroy us, if that system is disassembled, what then? Who are the "we?" Does the direction that we move forward to have to be a collective decision, and if not what are the parameters of equitable decision making? We discuss revolutions but not how or in what ways after deconstruction, what we do after that. What is the plan, the architecture, the blueprint? For dreams to be actualized we must plan and be informed by our communities and move forward with work as if we know that defined dream is going to happen. If we lack a plan post revolution or if the revolution shows its conviction without informed action as powerful as its rhetoric is, we detract from our movements.

How we value bodies within the United States context is contingent upon the capital we hold- socially, symbolically, and economically[87]. Our bodies are graded on how much power or capital the society within which we live extends to us based on its historical precedence. To divert from oppression Olympics, it must be stated that in trying to scaffold oppression, we place ourselves in a position wherein we position ourselves against one another within marginalized groups without building across movements. We must understand our unique systemic barriers, advocate with one another, and acknowledge the privileges we have. In ignoring these critical components of justice, we as the marginalized, plant and cultivate the same oppression we are a victim to. Not challenging oppression and oppressors collectively continue to turn the gears of oppression that leads to our demise. Without collectively confronting unique injustice we experience and attacking one another, the privileged gaze on us with satisfaction that their practice of oppression ostensibly removes fault from them. This removal of responsibility dilutes our power, and functions in a way wherein systemically the privileged don't have to be as explicit as to put chains on bo-

---

[87] Bourdieu, Pierre. "The forms of capital.(1986)." *Cultural theory: An anthology*(2011): 81-93.

dies. The privilege's tactics of destroying epistemology, demanding acculturation and expecting assimilation under its guides has put chains on our minds. This becomes evident when we don't understand one another's plights and move forward, together. Without interruption, without taking our minds back- we watch and experience oppression's continuance. As the system of oppression evolves and perfects itself, the historically privileged become immune to the process impacting the marginalized because these systems were designed to protect them.

Furthermore, it is difficult to talk about achievement or increased and retained economic capital for disenfranchised bodies when access was not extended (socially, economically, or politically) to past generations. This lack of extended access leaves a lack of room for transfer of wealth or equitable wealth distribution among the population. When we discuss libertarianism, we behave as if marginalized communities had not taken what they had and attempted to collectively build a form of sustainable vitality within their communities. It has been seen throughout history- Tulsa Oklahoma for example[88]- that economic capital achievement for marginalized community self-sufficiency in commerce has been met with tension, violence, and massacres. Privileged bodies felt a need to retain the sole ability to gain economic wealth had a goal of monopolizing the economy based on identities and a pathological need to control how a people survived or thrived. Therefore, these attempts of the marginalized to gain access to economic systems set in place for their self-sufficiency were consistently destroyed by hegemonic practices of power. Privileged bodies felt threatened by a commerce system that didn't need them to function[89]. Social consequences of racially charged rumors also made it so people of color, commerce and communities were also destroyed[90]. The dynamics of economics in an oppressive system is interesting wherein; privileged bodies accept and demand the money of those they disenfranchise while simultaneously rejecting their humanity. The systemic gatekeeping of access made this cruel expectation of spending economic capital

---

[88] Madigan, Tim. The burning: Massacre, destruction, and the Tulsa Race Riot of 1921. Macmillan, 2001.

[89] Greenwood, Ronni Michelle. "Remembrance, responsibility, and reparations: The use of emotions in talk about the 1921 Tulsa Race Riot." *Journal of Social Issues* 71, no. 2 (2015): 338-355.

[90] Jones, Maxine D. "The Rosewood Massacre and the Women Who Survived It." The Florida Historical Quarterly 76, no. 2 (1997): 193-208.

and being oppressed possible. Policies and social acceptance have allowed for this violence.

Nevertheless, we cannot again ignore that race was one of the most defining social forms of capitals that allow access within the Western framework of societal operation. Without the entrance on ramps of access through whiteness, one drift further from the ability to access or amass any power for self-efficacy whether they become complicit In the system's economic functions or not.

No amount of assimilation can get a body free, assimilation is a prison in and of itself. There may be some safety in assimilation. However, the amount of intergenerational trauma and the impacts that assimilation makes on the process of empowerment, hardly seems safe at all. Social capital also is extremely similar to cultural capital where in there is prestige in position. Without the component of particular identity "markers" of varying social capital - one can only go so far. When we discuss economic capital we have to have the conversation about how marginalized groups have not been able to gain access to it. We must account for history. Due to coercive migration, lack of citizenship, slavery, genocide, or being seen overall as less than- the libertarian bootstraps rhetoric is not at all applicable when discussing social mobility. We must take account of how that has impacted various generations though time[91].

Coercive Historical Placement

As previously discussed, coercive migration has again been one of this nation's most heinous approaches to fulfilling the ideology of Manifest Destiny, imperialism, and Darwinism[92].

From the moment of colonized infiltration, colonists forced Native and Indigenous populations of what is now known as the United States from their land. Colonizers set parameters for places in which the marginalized could live and readjusted those parameters at the will of those in power. These parameters were set within the nation state formed and deemed legitimate by those that laid claim to a land already inhabited without consultation or approval or significant recourse for their actions [93]. This was done with pure

---

[91] Feagin, Joe. *Systemic racism: A theory of oppression.* Routledge, 2013.

[92] Ninkovich, Frank. "The United States and Imperialism." *A Companion to American Foreign Relations* (2001): 79.

[93] Pommersheim, Frank. *Broken Landscape: Indians, Indian Tribes, and the Constitution.* Oxford University Press, 2009.

disregard for a people, their land, and their resources that made their ways of life possible in a holistic and interconnected manner. We also fail to discuss or elaborate on just how easy it was to rewrite villainous acts with a shifted narrative of heroics in textbooks and in media with representations such as "cowboys and Indians". How this would be villainized if it were any other nation that was being discussed and privileged bodies were the ones under siege. Transnational marginalization of an autonomous people. Yet we have the sheer gall to discuss immigration policies as if our manufactured way of life and obfuscated history would be threatened. But much like the African proverb states, "Until lions have their historians, tales of the hunt shall always glorify the hunter".

This type of hypocrisy falls in line with the expected absolution we will extend to ourselves despite our behavior, actions, and reprehensible ideologies. With these historical placements, we also continue to glide over the mass genocide of a people that was justified with rhetoric of barbarism. If someone was destroying your way of life with imperialistic practices- what other options are there but to resist in any form seen fit? How is transnational deceit and marginalization not defined as barbarism while self-defense for the marginalized is defined as such? Semantics and applicability thereof to bodies, matters.

Moving from this, the coercive placement of African and African American bodies has been a continuous operation of the United States from the time period of slavery to the "post-slavery" era. Even after slavery in its explicit form, the rights, movement as well as placement of black bodies has been directly dictated by policies. Slavery controlled what we ate, where we lived, who we procreated with, and was wrought with sexual abuses and psychological trauma that ingrained itself in our physiology[94]. When the patriarchal model was implemented, it was made clear that black males would not have the ability to participate in that system. But that does not save us from people within marginalized communities behaving as if the system of oppression would benefit them. This furthers the psychological cycle of planting destruction based practices into a population by proxy. We have to weed these practices out. We also often behave as if those within our own communities should be maligned

---

[94] Sullivan, Shannon. *The Physiology of Sexist and Racist Oppression*. Oxford University Press, 2015.

by the same social statutes that were placed on us. How is that going to get anyone free?

After slavery, Jim Crow laws perpetuated the psychological and physical placement of African Americans where movement and placement was solely based on the color of our skin through segregation and anti-miscegenation protocols[95]. Black women's bodies were seen as property for any white body to take ownership of in a de facto sense, especially when work within a capitalistic system was used as leverage for work such as domesticity. The result was multitudes of black women raising white families while white families behaved as if the care given to their children was more important than the importance of black mothers raising their own children. These were mothers who cared for other people's children that had to find time to care for their own.[96]

As for males, it was very clear that the country still didn't want black males to participate in any dimensions of a patriarchal system. This was so, unless it perpetuated white supremacist practices of oppression thereby retaining control over those that perpetuated the practice. In a capitalistic society, black males were rarely given work, furthering their marginalization. This furthered the black family from being able to participate in the designed economic system of this country. Black males were commonly emasculated within a patriarchal society. They were also feeding into relative depravation that catalyzed practicing learned oppression based tactics on their own community. The colonial system was never design for bodies once deemed as property to compete economically or to retain property or assets. Systemic barriers solidified that premise from the pretext of historical marginalization and African Americans were barred from competing with hegemony. During and after slavery, black families were impacted in an extremely negative way and black people were forced to put the pieces back together.

After the emancipation proclamation, there were various efforts to return African Americans to Africa but by this time, psychologically so much of their history and culture was taken away from

---

[95] Woods, Jeff R. *Black Struggle, Red Scare: Segregation and Anti-Communism in the South, 1948--1968*. LSU Press, 2003.

[96] Fox-Genovese, Elizabeth. Within the plantation household: Black and white women of the old south. UNC Press Books, 2000.

them[97]. They were now considered African Americans with a limited if any memory of Africa. Understanding where their lineage
was actually from had been taken away- What would they be returning to? Some led initiatives for black people to get back to their
roots but epistemology or lack thereof wasn't going to make that
process easy or less painful. Others supported initiatives of bodies
to return to Africa because without the utility of slavery, hegemonic
groups feared the consequences they may be met with from freed
slaves. Some just wanted black bodies to be eradicated from society
if they couldn't be controlled or be seen as free labor functioning
property[98]. Those who pushed these initiatives did not take this into
account but more so wanted to reap the benefits of a nation being
constructed on the backs of slave labor wanted to rid themselves
from African American presence now that they could not legally
enslave them. I do realize these paragraphs exist in binary format.
However, we have limited information on those who identified as
non-binary and this information held also does not discuss ability
or transgender identities with racially marginalized that were coercively migrated from this era[99].

From seeing ideological notions become crystallized in actions,
practice, and policies, we must also take a moment to discuss how
historical placement has something to do with social capital when
we discuss colorism. Through certain efforts such as the paper bag
test[100] or how we see beauty- all these concepts and practices thereof are based on Eurocentric valuations of beauty and acceptability. It is true that there were consensual interracial relationships and
that some racially passed for safety, but there were also many who
were and are raped, sexually assaulted and harassed, and many
who passed to gain social mobility[101]. We must also recognize that
we talk about beauty in reference to women as if It is the only currency they have; to be commodified or gain entry into a space. We

[97] Guelzo, Allen C. *Lincoln's Emancipation Proclamation: The End of Slavery in America.* Simon and Schuster, 2005.
[98] Smitherman, Geneva. "" What Is Africa to Me?": Language, Ideology, and African American." American Speech 66, no. 2 (1991): 115-132.
[99] Richardson, Matt. The Queer Limit of Black Memory: Black Lesbian Litera-ture and Irresolution. Columbus: Ohio State University Press, 2013.
[100] Kerr, Audrey Elisa. *The Paper Bag Principle: Class, colorism, and rumor and the case of Black Washington.* Univ. of Tennessee Press, 2006.
[101] Harper, Phillip Brian. "Passing for what? Racial masquerade and the demands of upward mobility." Callaloo 21, no. 2 (1998): 381-397.

need not in marginalized groups repeat these oppressive cognitive processes of beauty standards within our own communities. It does not benefit us, and moreover, it divides our efficacy, dilutes self-agency, autonomy, and our collective power in ways that reinforce the intention of beauty standard baselines in the first place. To look to society to approve your body, pay the price of that approval, and as a society it stops us from defining beauty for ourselves. We must also interrupt ourselves from seeing the word beauty as a gendered concept. This too reinforces patriarchal practice in damaging ways to masculine of center and non-binary people. Why can femme essence on a man not be beautiful? Why can masculinity not be beautiful? Why do we feel the need to meet the use or presence of femininity or words assumed to be in relation to it with over compensatory masculinity when it is not directed at a cisgender female? Why do we use the word beauty as if it something we have to wait to be called to discern our worth instead of just telling ourselves that we are beautiful every day?

It is important to state that often, the way color is being discussed will be on a polarized aspect (black and white). We must too understand that, historically, the closer we align to whiteness which is improperly used as a baseline of "normalcy" determines how we can navigate society and what gates will open within it. What is important to note is where our bodies are physically or socially placed and how that placement is determined by how visible our transgressions are from that able bodied white male and male gazed defined "normal" baseline.

The United States has constantly threatened to or continues to colonize domestically and abroad in a physical, emotional, and mental dimension. In the realm of militarization in a land of "free will"- we instituted a draft that demanded where bodies must be[102]. When we have this discussion, it is typically quelled with a digressing narrative of what falls into the rubric of "Americanism and patriotism"[103]. In this recognition, a person has two options. The first option is to freely exist as promised in the constitution and be met with punitive repercussions such as criminalization and surveil-

---

[102] Lutz, Catherine. "Making war at home in the United States: Militarization and the current crisis." *American Anthropologist* 104, no. 3 (2002): 723-735.

[103] Foley, Michael S. *Confronting the war machine: Draft resistance during the Vietnam War.* Univ of North Carolina Press, 2003.

lance. The other option is to give up one's freedom to a cause that typically in all of its complexity can be reduced a complete contrast of the narrative being pushed to society through its process of mandatory recruitment. Even beyond the draft, the actual fact that Congress and the Executive branch have the power to place politics on an individual's bodies is disturbing. There is no consultation, just expected capitulation. This is not a critique of those who join the military for whatever reasons they deemed appropriate, but a critique of militarization and the processes to which it abides by that takes agency away from a body. When we think about military tactics, the United States is often credited with liberating Jewish populations within German captured lands. The relative truth is that we didn't get involved in World War II until the bombing of Pearl Harbor[104]. This consequence could be rationalized as a justified reason for retaliation. However, we cannot behave as if we did not turn our backs on the disenfranchisement of the Jewish people years before and that our focus was notably retaliatory efforts towards the Japanese government[105]. Through that retaliation, we killed countless human beings ourselves. We are not as humanitarian as we claim or pride ourselves on being. We make ourselves feel better by discussing casualties of civilian vs. military personnel, but a life is a life and has meaning. We also have to understand that we all are socialized, we all join factions for different reasons and we all are at the mercy of our nation's directives until we decide we don't want to be. From this, tragedies are inevitable and we really don't know why we're fighting anyone and struggling to live a dignified life within our own borders at the same time. This can be seen based on the way we treated Japanese Americans during World War II. In what way can we tout liberation of a people? We enslave people, intern people, deport people, and detain people because of their identities- we tout our embodiment of freedom but we have far more mechanisms for enslavement and control than we do for anything that remotely mirrors liberation[106]. Police or military force is often used in tandem with the tool of fear as a form of bandwagon effect inducting persuasion for marginalized groups to be treated with ac-

---

[104] Chafe, William Henry. *The Unfinished Journey: America Since World War II*. Oxford University Press, USA, 2003.

[105] Mueller, John, and Karl Mueller. "Sanctions of mass destruction." *Foreign Affairs* (1999): 43-53.

[106] Daniels, Roger. *Prisoners Without Trial: Japanese Americans in World War II*. Macmillan, 2004.

cepted oppression. From women, to people of color to queer populations, to varying abilities, to queer people of color with disabili-
ties- fear of contagion is a tool used to rationale asinine ideologies
and oppressive practices thereof.

   In the arena of documentation and what makes a citizen- we reduce humanity, freedom to move, and access for a human being to
pieces of paper. We however have historically exploited a marginalized people and then demand they leave or force them into political and ontological subservience. We have done it with African
Americans. When many remained, the tactics to make life unbeara-
ble was hoped to breed acquiesces or repatriation, but with what
compensation, resources, retribution or reparations? When the
Chinese were employed and paid disproportionately, the United
States decided that they did not want more Chinese populations
coming into the nation and not returning back to their homeland.
With this, we pushed forward policies such as the Chinese Exclusion Act[107] and the Nordic Act[108] . These acts only favored Western
European migration. For a short moment of time the Irish Catholics
were also seen as less than in comparison to the White Angle-Saxon
Protestants (WASPs). This soon shifted as the demographics were
clearly changing due to migration of people of color and to retain
the power and force of whiteness- the Irish subsequently became
white.[109]

   Now at present day we must continue to discuss the ways in
which undocumented persons are treated. We must again make it
clear that as a society we have heavily racialized the issue of migration and in doing so we imply the acceptability and the humanity of
those that they migrate from Western European nations[110]. As we
proceed with the racialized immigration conversation in the national context, it has almost completely diverted to "concern" over
the Mexican and Muslim population and those assumed to identify

---

[107] Congress, By. "Chinese Exclusion Act." In *47th Congress, Session I.* 1882.
[108] Ngai, Mae M. "The architecture of race in American immigration law: A
      reexamination of the Immigration Act of 1924." *The Journal of Ameri-
      can History* 86, no. 1 (1999): 67-92.
[109] Ignatiev, Noel. *How the Irish became white.* Routledge, 2009
[110] Ngai, Mae M. "The architecture of race in American immigration law: A
      reexamination of the Immigration Act of 1924." *The Journal of Ameri-
      can History* 86, no. 1 (1999): 67-92.

with the aforementioned groups[111]. This phenomenon is one that is difficult to discuss as many try to state it's not about race- wen we know that it is. We see that it is and we witness the impacts of that truth. These implicitly racialized conversations demonize groups, communities of people, and a bandwagon effect lacking rationality has again come to the fore..

When we discuss immigration and refugee status, we understand the means by which United States has practiced its self-proclamation as police of the world with its tactics of national security endorsement in conjunction with the United Nations[112]. The nuances of humanitarianism emerge from the dynamics domestically, transnationally, and on a global context. After the "War on Terror" commenced[113], hypervigilance and vigilantism extended towards people of color and their bodies become battle grounds of suspected criminalization to an even higher degree than it already existed[114]. It is worth questioning if these bodies migrating were of Western European descent would the resistance argument be present, and would it be the same? Would we associate the term "terrorism" with actions perpetrated by people of European dissent transnationally the way that fail to domestically? I'm not... arguing that defence tactics should never be used. But, we must notably identify that the term terror or terrorism is rarely, if ever used on bodies of western European background- we have to consistently call out these incongruences. Terrorism does not have color and it is absurd to assign a color and race, or ethnicity to the term's applicability.

The issue with immigration and with marginalized populations- is that if this nation "gives you a chance" it always comes at a price. By this I mean it extends to you basic human rights found in its "foundational" documents, but the United States expect one to be

---

[111] Rouse, Roger. "Mexican migration and the social space of postmodernism." *Diaspora: a journal of transnational Studies* 1, no. 1 (1991): 8-23.

[112] Bush, George W. *The national security strategy of the United States of America.* EXECUTIVE OFFICE OF THE PRESIDENT WASHINGTON DC, 2002.

[113] Bhattacharyya, Gargi S. *Dangerous brown men: exploiting sex, violence and feminism in the'war on terror'.* Zed, 2008.

[114] Tirman, John. "Immigration and insecurity: post-9/11 fear in the United States." *MIT Center for International Studies Audit of the Conventional Wisdom* (2006): 06-09.

an exemplary model citizen with no human error[115]. All the while, we ignore the fact that no one can be exemplary model citizen that is already here, so why would we in policy or in social expectations demand that someone be superhuman? There's a difference between self determination to migrate and expected subservience because citizenship or entrance into this country is granted or achieved. Considering deportation- the entire system should be abolished. There are those who have been taken to detention centers and then to prisons and been completely lost within the system[116]. There are families being broken apart and children that have to go into foster care. There are people who are simply living their lives and exercising their right to breathe that are being villainized based on some Western Imaginary we all adhere to of arbitrary borders.[117] Though borders are imaginary, they are also nuanced in how they are very real and have very real implications for particular bodies, especially as the notion of immigration has continuously been racialized and attacked. Who gives these borders control over our body? How and why do land lines fundamentally dictate how free our bodies could be?

The associations of "othering" extends not only across border lines but we have domesticized the practice within the United States alone in gentrification and redlining dynamics and practices tantamount to border lines that separate countries in that they disregard humanity, access, and mobility through intentional marginalization[118]. After slavery ended, the United States put considerable effort into not allowing the votes of the marginalized to count in ways that could sway the overall outcome of the "democratic" process[119]. Therefore, African Americans were redistricted and remanded to live in particular neighborhoods. It became a legal

---

[115] Gupta, Monisha Das. *Unruly immigrants: Rights, activism, and transnational South Asian politics in the United States.* Duke University Press, 2006.

[116] Kalhan, Anil. "Rethinking immigration detention." *Colum. L. Rev. Sidebar* 110 (2010): 42.

[117] Bhagwati, Jagdish. "Borders beyond control." *Foreign Aff.* 82 (2003): 98.

[118] Christensen, Linda. "Rethinking Research: Reading and Writing about the Roots of Gentrification." *English Journal* 105, no. 2 (2015): 15.

[119] Waymer, Damion, and Robert L. Heath. "Black Voter Dilution, American Exceptionalism, and Racial Gerrymandering The Paradox of the Positive in Political Public Relations." *Journal of Black Studies* (2016): 0021934716649646.

statute that one did not have to rent, sell, or allow loan approvals to create businesses for racially marginalized groups in many areas[120]. What is so harrowing about this process is that it was allowed to happen and that it actually worked with minimal interruption. With the lack of business loans or home ownership, there could be no social or economic mobility. With home loans, people could only live in particular areas with minimal voting power, and the schools' fiscal government disbursement of funds was based on the property tax of that area[121] . This limited the scope of what was generally attainable from resources. Student teacher ratios were also hindered and impacted the possibility of optimized learning environments. We have been making clear how much bodies have been valued and devalued in this chapter and property is no exception. The value of a property based on the demographics of a neighborhood has nothing to do with square footage and everything to do with the color of one's skin that inhabits the neighborhood. Previously, we discussed the ability to survive vs. thrive- with gentrification, bodies have been displaced into areas where there are considerable food and health desserts and without concern these processes continue[122]. Though these practices are now met with more question, the vociferousness of the people has not shaken these practices and many people of marginalized identities are forced to go out of their neighborhood for essential needs. Marginalized populations have to spend their resources elsewhere and travel back home to an area that will never benefit from their commerce[123]. Sound familiar? History repeats itself if we don't interrupt it form doing as such.

The stereotypes of the lazy black body, the "anchor baby", the violent, the mentally inept, etc. continues to extend among marginalized populations and rarely or barely affects or impacts those who

---

[120] Yinger, John. *Closed doors, opportunities lost: The continuing costs of housing discrimination.* Russell Sage Foundation, 1995.

[121] Boustan, Leah, Fernando Ferreira, Hernan Winkler, and Eric M. Zolt. "The effect of rising income inequality on taxation and public expenditures: Evidence from US municipalities and school districts, 1970–2000." *Review of Economics and Statistics* 95, no. 4 (2013): 1291-1302.

[122] Walker, Renee E., Christopher R. Keane, and Jessica G. Burke. "Disparities and access to healthy food in the United States: A review of food deserts literature." *Health & place* 16, no. 5 (2010): 876-884.

[123] Slater, Tom. "Looking at the" North American city" through the lens of gentrification discourse." *Urban Geography* 23, no. 2 (2002): 131-153.

share the common denominator of whiteness. I do not say this haphazardly because it is with the understanding that women, those with varying abilities and those in the LGBTQQIA2S+ community do experience marginalization, stereotype, and stigma. All these marginalized groups have and continue to be disenfranchised. We must make clear that the compounded effects of holding multiple minority intersections defined by Crenshaw at the crux of race[124], renders us invisible. This invisibility increasingly makes the marginalized more disposable and from this there is no safety within any space of one's identity. For instance, in the realm of gender and sexuality, how many trans women of color have been killed by violence? How many women of color report sexual assault and are met with no assistance? How many lower income multiple marginalized groups are denied access to our society and the protections it claims to offer, how many domestic violence calls were ignored among LGBTQ+ populations of color? The compounded effects of being a woman of color is of a heavy weight despite ability or sexuality. The importance here lies in how we consistently devalue the acumen of women and how we fail to advocate for their concerns, most importantly sexual assault and proper compensation. We continually make excuses for perpetrators' behavior and question the mental capacity of women under the notion of hysteria to which we still use to diminish the character of women today[125]. Now take into consideration, the race based conversation held in previous sections. Intersectionality holds a heavy weight. At each marginalized convergence, we see how precariousness and barriers of these intersections meet at nexus that exists millimeters away from a navigable move that could result in bending or breaking.

Residual Impacts

It is evident that what was set forth by colonization did not stop, because it never ceased in practice only in the name by which it is called. Colonization of body, land and mind, were practiced and is practiced without caution for the aftermath to society, and it operates solely to benefit the privileged. Therefore, it is important to

---

[124] Crenshaw, Kimberle. "Mapping the margins: Intersectionality, identity politics, and violence against women of color." *Stanford law review* (1991): 1241-1299.

[125] Ussher, Jane M. "Diagnosing difficult women and pathologising femininity: Gender bias in psychiatric nosology." *Feminism & Psychology* 23, no. 1 (2013): 63-69.

bring attention to the question of what exactly are the inherently residual impacts of colonialist methodologies and agendas.

When we look at marginalized populations, intersections in tow, it becomes evident that colonist agendas have wholeheartedly infused itself in the veins of our lifelines within the United States. From institutions to the idea that clothing equals competence in respectability politics, and the notice that hegemonic entitlement extends a right to take or discard a body without much support to challenge that form of social acceptance- cyclical oppression is clear. We continue to devalue black and brown bodies, women, people of varying abilities, various sexualities and gender identities. These marginalizations are based on social constructions of race, gender, sexuality, documentation status, and ability that have had residual implications that cannot be done away with, with any policy. Systems have made it difficult to achieve any additional shifts. Due to the policy amendment's failure to name the specific affected bodies and practices that negatively impact marginalized groups in ways that catalyze the continued pushback an actual deconstruction of the dynamics that destroy us, we fail to identify the roots of our policies in ways that the nation can compute in present day.

We create policies to protect black bodies from discrimination[126], however as can be seen in the criminal justice system, these abhorrent actions of violence towards black bodies rarely find justice[127]. Yes, we are judged in what seems to be a stable system, but this is the same system that perpetuated and stabilized the institutionalization of –isms. As black and brown bodies are criminalized we see the residual impacts of colonization with disproportionate sentencing and police harassment. These disproportionate consequences along with interpersonal and individual biases grow exponentially as the "justice" system makes clear who can actually obtain justice. This is not an instance for only black and brown bodies as can be seen with women of all races that report sexual assault, harassment or discrimination encounter a massive lack of justice[128.]

---

[126] Crenshaw, Kimberle. "Demarginalizing the intersection of race and sex: A black feminist critique of antidiscrimination doctrine, feminist theory and antiracist politics." U. Chi. Legal F. (1989): 139.

[127] Lee, Cynthia. "Making race salient: Trayvon Martin and implicit bias in a not yet post-racial society." (2013).

[128] Tjaden, Patricia, and Nancy Thoennes. "Prevalence, Incidence, and Consequences of Violence against Women: Findings from the National Violence against Women Survey. Research in Brief." (1998).

We detain and dehumanize as a product of our Western framework of mind. In some type of phenomenological direction, we
choose to not acknowledge this disproportionality among black and
brown queer populations, women, or men[129]. It is interesting that
an anecdote is not enough and is reduced as inconsequential, when
it is continuously brought to the fore that these anecdotes are not
unique. Even with statistical information to discuss pay gaps,
there's a refutation of the data to maintain the status quo thought
process that our system actually works[130]. So when is data accepted,
when are stories accepted by hegemony? We have to wonder why at
some point- are we trying to convince or "prove" what we as a
community already know is valid. When we acknowledge that historically to present, hegemonic groups aren't going to do anything
about disenfranchisement or admit to it fully, why do we keep expecting them to? What are we expecting them to do that we can't in
time do ourselves? Is this the peaceful process, where marginalized
communities continue to be disenfranchised and die while a few
hearts and mind may change but are accompanied by no action?
We have to spend more time thinking about who will, what will, and
what can be done. These questions must be asked unless we are just
waiting for who we deem to be the right representatives to advocate
for the marginalized. However, the way the system operates- I can't
with confidence say that's ever going to happen the way we dream.

The residual impacts of colonization go much further that gentri-
fying displacement in present day. Our optics are continuously
skewed by colonialist rhetoric and conversely, we have been made
well aware of the price of resistance. Throughout history of the 20th
and the 21st century there has been considerable resistance and
many would believe that a resolution is possible. The residual impact of knowing a system was not set up for certain bodies to thrive
becomes important as we design our continuance forward. Following the Polybian cycle of monarchy, aristocracy, democracy, mob
rule and anarchy- we try to discern the price of a revolution and ask
ourselves if it is something we have the willingness to proceed with[131].

---

[129] Cole, David. No equal justice: Race and class in the American criminal
justice system. The New Press, 1999.

[130] Amott, Teresa L., and Julie A. Matthaei. *Race, gender, and work: A multicultural economic history of women in the United States.* South End
Press, 1996.

[131] Fleisher, Martin. "The ways of Machiavelli and the ways of politics." *History of Political Thought* 16, no. 3 (1995): 330-355.

In understanding that residual impacts still stain our way of life, in mental health and physical disability (visible or invisible) we have come to an understanding that a simple policy being put in place does not get to the root of the problem. Creating the American Disability Act (ADA) still allows spaces to do the bare minimum with systems as "reasonable accommodation" bend left to subjectivity[132]. Affirmative action also does not structure itself in a way that repercussions are expected if an employer doesn't equitably practice it[133]. After all, how do you "prove" discrimination? Overall, anti-discrimination clauses create the acknowledgement of diversity's importance but many marginalized still experience discrimination, that is difficult to "fix" if their rights are infringed upon. The burden of proof is nearly impossible to obtain because we have been socialized to be implicit[134]. Now, as religious exemption has surfaced itself as a defense mechanism to protect discriminatory practices, it has become extremely difficult for many marginalized persons to navigate.[135]

Why people need an excuse to discriminate is bewildering, but maybe the reduction of that conversation comes down to people not wanting to make accommodations for identities they don't hold and that they don't want to be told what to do. Should a new system be implemented because ours doesn't work? What would be the price of that transformation? We stated before that human beings are capable of rationalization. However, the fruit that our minds bear find it difficult to utilize our neuroplasticity to shift our culture or is at the least, unwilling to try. One thing to note is that the systems that were instituted by which we live in accordance with did exactly what they were intended to do - retain power for a select group of people. However, we have never lived within a true social-

---

[132] Waterstone, Michael. "Untold Story of the Rest of the Americans with Disabilities Act, The." *Vand. L. Rev.* 58 (2005): 1807.

[133] Coate, Stephen, and Glenn C. Loury. "Will affirmative-action policies eliminate negative stereotypes?" *The American Economic Review* (1993): 1220-1240.

[134] Bartholet, Elizabeth. "Proof of Discriminatory Intent Under Title VII: United States Postal Service Board of Governors v. Aikens." *California Law Review* 70, no. 5 (1982): 1201-1220.

[135] Curtis, Michael Kent. "A Unique Religious Exemption from Antidiscrimination Laws in the Case of Gays? Putting the Call for Exemptions for Those Who Discriminate Against Married or Marrying Gays in Context." In *The Rule of Law and the Rule of God*, pp. 83-114. Palgrave Macmillan US, 2014.

ist based democracy. Maybe we should try to actualize what that could look like. Often times in history we use terms and shift their conceptualization. At its purest forms we don't live in a socialist system where taxes are appropriately balanced with social services that allow for social mobility, but some modified bastardization of what it could turn into if a few pieces of the rubric of its definition are fulfilled.

Residuals are so important to dissect- and we cannot continue to behave as if our systems were truly what they ever stated they could be for all people, nor can we explain that we are some exemplary model of how a government should function. There are residual impacts felt de facto among populations of color, LGBTQQIA2S+ populations, women, and those with varying abilities and we have to acknowledge that. Women are still seen as inferior and each sexist commentary reinforces the disposability of femininity. This disposability is practiced despite the contrary strength that women hold. Queerness is continuously bashed and demonized and a direct victim of religious exemption based excuses. Marginalized populations overall are continuously dismissed when the sanctity of their bodies are violated with violence, verbal harassment, male or racial entitlement or white nationalism. The residuals of colonization are the continuation of the practice under the veil of different fabricated concepts and their ever-changing definitions.

Despite the oppression placed on bodies and its residual impacts, marginalized populations within the United States have found a way to find joy no matter how many times its presence is few, far, and in between. For the fact that cultures can and have been created is an homage the strength of marginalized people. However, the places that we do thrive are either in clandestine safe or safer spaces or in precarious "public" spaces that are often times surveilled. There is also a residual impact within creating our own cultures that holds the cultures created despite oppression in music, in speech, in dance, in walk, in family ties that exudes an intergenerational story and pulse. All of these things are a result of surviving and thriving when one can under pressure of oppression. Finding mediums of liberation, more often than not however comes with a culture being co-opted, components of a marginalized culture are often co-opted and appropriated by the Westernized frame with no credit under the "melting pot" rhetoric. While these appropriated cultural practices gain legitimacy, visibility, and benignity among the privileged as they imitate it, society in turn denounces and disparages these cultural affects and components and expressions thereof when the cultures' creators live within and exercise their *own* culture[136].

The main residual impact of colonized practices and mindsets are that it stops marginalized populations from imagining or actualizing "full time" freedom. Maybe when we discuss the term freedom we always have meant it in a conditional way.

With the privatization of prisons and the theft of voting rights, we know that the disproportionality of low income people of color is astronomical in comparison to the affluence or social capital of whiteness. The system of economic disparity has long lasting consequences[137]. I don't say this in a way that minimizes the lack of access for those of low income overall. However, identity politics come into play when we decide who perceptually receives empathy and who perceptually receives persecution through accusation in ways that become common place stereotypes that in turn are applied to a people. Economic disparity is a structural strategy that retains power with those who hold identities that were not barred from fiscal access and participation in the systems of capitalism. I don't continuously bring up the term capitalism as if it an amazing frontier that we should all enter. I am, though, highlighting how capitalism is directly connected as a used tool of white heteropatriarchal oppression practices in the United States. This topic must be integrated into the conversation when we discuss systemic dynamics of access and economic capital's power.

Society at large would like to believe that now residual impacts are not present because we don't see outright hostility in public spaces as much as historical images of –isms that we are familiar with seeing. However, microinvalidation and mircoaggressions are forms of oppression, sexism, ableism, racism, and heterosexism. Its violence is performed in ways that people are rarely called out or called in on because of its insidiousness and we fail as a society to recognize and interrupt those circumventing behaviors that perpetuate oppression. People with membership to hegemonic groups perpetuate these "–isms" without realizing their impacts. While this perpetuation continues, those exercising multiple consciousnesses become

---

[136] Young, James O., and Conrad G. Brunk. *The ethics of cultural appropriation.* John Wiley & Sons, 2012.

[137] Dawson, Hannah. "Do they look like me?: Rethinking representation and its relationship with freedom." *Juncture* 21, no. 2 (2014): 136-139.

exhausted of their options to interrupt, educate, or endure. These options do not guarantee that their articulation of these impacts will be believed, validated, or met aggressively.

In what can be seemingly reduced to insignificant, the residual impact of the colonialism of the mind and land is the way that we perpetuate the colorism of imagery. We dilute the potency of crime with words such as "white" lie or "white collared crime", minimizing the impacts it receives for fundamentally breaking a law, and telling a lie. We find ways to apply these terms to bodies and those who practice these infractions scathe away virtually untouched in ways that favor a privileged class of people [138]. We treat those with bodies that go further on the spectrum of color toward brown and black with the disdain that the nation has always placed on the meanings of words, and color. In this- bodies that have been placed into the social construction bear the brunt of their implications. We teach the process of color association and act accordingly socially and politically without pause. We discussed before how we scale body value based on how close color is to blackness or whiteness. We understand that others of marginalized races identify within the spectrum and are treated on varying scales of acceptability or disposability because of it. Understanding this on the degreed presence or absence of melanin, it must be stated that we have placed this on the way that we understand the rhetoric of imagery. We in the Westernized state of being have demonized the dark and overly glorified the light. In a way, this rhetoric has become a way we internalized the worth of ourselves and the worth we see in others. If the word darkness or blackness is often seen as sullen, spoiled, evil and whiteness is always seen as pure or positive- in what ways do you think we are going to understand ourselves and those we see in our society? The impact of imagery is subliminal and becomes ontological. It takes much work to shift that narrative. Narratives are ingrained in the way we understand, the way we speak, and the ways we are to interpret what we see in others as well as ourselves. This will be further discussed in the media chapter but needed to be uplifted in the section that discusses residual impacts as well.

It is easy enough to become inoculated to the expectations of normalcy. When we take steps back to what this baseline of normalcy has done to our society, we realize even on what can be consi-

---

[138] Reiman, Jeffrey, and Paul Leighton. *The rich get richer and the poor get prison: Ideology, class, and criminal justice.* Routledge, 2015.

dered to be the smallest of levels, it pervades. marginalized lives and the particular expectations placed on them causes considerable detriment to lives being fully lived. One example that can be used would be color. We talked earlier about colorism and the imagery of darkness and light but for a moment let us move away solely discussing race. We can also make space to discuss what this means for gender, gender expression, and sexuality. Again, we are dealing with another type of dichotomous binary when we think about what is traditionally understood to be blue and pink, respectability for what color is for a boy and what color is for a girl. Not taking into consideration that intersex is a sex and that non-gender conforming bodies have a historical presence within our cultures. We don't take time to understand that gender binaries should not exist or be directly correlated to the sex assigned at birth. The expectations when entering the world comes with demands on bodies before the first cry of a newborn even ceases. Furthermore, when people identify with the sex they have been assigned, that doesn't categorically mean that they favor things that fit into the dichotomous binary of what is boyish and what is girlish. When preferences are identified that fall outside the guides of gender role theory, society ostracizes developing youth for their free thought in attempt to make them "normal"[139]. If colors are picked that are associated with masculinity for those assigned female at birth there is a little more leeway in their criticism than when colors or things associated with those colors by expectation extend to femininity for those assigned male at birth. This also is a direct example of how a color can dictate the safety that we have in society and it also makes clear the devaluation we have for anything we deem feminine[140]. There remains a strong belief that there is no power or strength within femininity. Femininity, masculinity or androgyny doesn't belong to any particular sex or gender. We must realize that all of these gender expression traits can be embodied by anybody regardless of identity. People should have the autonomy to hold and project these expressions without the threat of violence or being barred social safety efficacy or mobility and remove the associations that society correlates to a body that favors something as simple as a color. When we

---

[139] Ridgeway, Cecilia L., and Shelley J. Correll. "Unpacking the gender system a theoretical perspective on gender beliefs and social relations." *Gender & society* 18, no. 4 (2004): 510-531.

[140] Bartky, Sandra Lee. *Femininity and domination: Studies in the phenomenology of oppression.* Psychology Press, 1990.

make light of strong arguments being made that discuss how what is considered to be "harmless" begets violence, we need to take a moment to understand how minimizing dismissal of these imagery topics directly affects the way someone can navigate within society. This extends to toys, books, extracurricular activities- all because of expectations and demands of reinforcing what is normal with no justifiable cause for its rationalization[141].

There have been moments where we demand that toys be in particular colors to make identifiers of who should and who should not have these things[142]. We have arguments on Fox News with reporters over the color over the color of Santa Claus when children seek representation that meets backlash (when he isn't real)[143]. When we don't allow for the freedom to break the mold of compulsory expectations of normalcy - we are literally ruining people's lives before they can even speak and taking liberty away from them.

Fearing the Oppressed (Retention of Power)

I'm certain we can't continue using the terms postcolonial and I'm not certain that the term neocolonialism is appropriate when we discuss body value, or control. There's nothing neo- beyond the expression of circumvention about its practice. These colonialist practices continue to invade and rule our perception of the land we live on and the mind frames by which we perceive and process our environments. The more marginalized populations increase their self-efficacy and ability to navigate through an oppressive system despite its barricades, the more anxiety this induces among privileged populations and the byproducts of that anxiousness continues to surface in violence in all of its forms, much like the past.

Do those that hold undeniable privilege resent the possible freedom of those once marginalized? The only explanation, if this is true, that can be given to this perception is fear. This fear of the oppressed goes much further than economic shifts in sharing power, but reaches over into various forms and dimensions of violence

---

[141] Foss, Sonja K., Mary E. Domenico, and Karen A. Foss. *Gender stories: Negotiating identity in a binary world.* Waveland Press, 2012.

[142] Foss, Sonja K., Mary E. Domenico, and Karen A. Foss. *Gender stories: Negotiating identity in a binary world.* Waveland Press, 2012.

[143] Copenhaver-Johnson, Jeane F., Joy T. Bowman, and Angela C. Johnson. "Santa stories: Children's inquiry about race during picturebook read-alouds." *Language Arts* 84, no. 3 (2007): 234-244.

and surveillance. There is still a perceived feeling that the privileged need to hold power over a groups to retain power. It is propelled by stereotypes and stigmas extended generationally. When the suffragist movement achieved its goal for white women- the idea of free thought for women was met with commentary that they could not be protected, that women were too mentally fragile to make decisions for our nation. However, the fear has always been free thought at its core, especially seeing that women overpopulated men[144]. This befuddles the practice of majority vs. minority and actualizes these words in terms correlative to supremacy. Without reigns being placed on people in forms of dehumanization, the ability to think freely would give way to the ability within even a modified system of democracy, to shift the culture. Sadly, because of the way that the suffragist movement bifurcated when it came to race, what it was capable of was not what it achieved and whiteness prevailed over color instead of creating a unified front toward injustice[145]. When we leave bodies out of social justice movements due to the socio-political climate, the rhetoric of "not yet", or that society isn't ready is often used. While this rhetoric is used, those that are marginalized continue to be marginalized with the absence of advocacy. As we socially perpetuate that practice of leaving people behind that we never return to get, we make clear our values that align to supremacist practices and in this we become no ideologically different than our own oppressors.

After slavery there were so many policies set in place to control black bodies[146] and why is this? Is it because we fear the oppressed with the thought process that those who have intergenerationally been oppressed will treat those who oppressed them the way that they have and are being treated? There's never been a chance to determine what freedom within a system could look like because those in power will not allow for its possibility. A larger question is that if fear fuels the privilege's concern, why would they think that historical forms of oppression were the only ways that the marginalized would implement liberation based change? Having a lack of epistemology beyond the Western mind frame for those who have

---

[144] Rothenberg, Paula S. *Race, class, and gender in the United States: An integrated study*. Macmillan, 2004.

[145] Crawford, Elizabeth. *The Women's Suffrage Movement: A Reference Guide 1866-1928*. Routledge, 2003.

[146] Roberts, Dorothy. *Killing the black body: Race, reproduction, and the meaning of liberty*. Vintage, 2014.

been burdened by it for so long does call issues to question, but instead of having the conversation, we vehemently avoid it and this reifies the perception that the marginalized cannot be innovative in deconstructing oppression.

When we discuss power, it has been stated several times that we don't know how to share it. The only time power has been distributed has been among those deemed the elite. However, to determine pathways to share power with all people is something that should be further discussed. Why is sharing power such a marvel of an idea in theoretical conversation yet on a greater macro scale, the ability to determine how to make that ideology work continues to live in purgatory. It will always be difficult to give up power, even if we did nothing to have it- our color, ability, sexuality, gender, citizenship status, are all forms of cultural and social capital if we align with Western hegemony. Absolutely nothing was done to gain those privileges in most cases yet we are begrudged when asked to share its power and fall back on the argument that we "earned" something as if our inequitable capital did not help us achieve our strides. With sharing power, we also place ourselves in a situation where we have to release control again that we claim we don't have over a people. What about not being in control of someone else is so bothersome? Whatever the response is, no group of people should have power or control over the autonomy and freedom of another on the most fundamental level- so why do we allow this to continue?

How can we as a society continue to let people fall back on a victimization narrative when they possess identities that extend them the ability to be free? Many marginalized have paid the price for resisting simply for the possibility of autonomy and freedom.[147] What is more troubling, is that much like economics and cost burdens, what we find a way to pay for doesn't mean we can afford it. We must also understand that simply because different forms of freedom are available, does not mean it is accessible for and to everyone due to structural barriers. This is why the notion of equity is so important.

---

[147] Fletcher, Laurel E., and Harvey M. Weinstein. "Violence and social repair: Rethinking the contribution of justice to reconciliation." *Human Rights Quarterly* 24, no. 3 (2002): 573-639.

With politics, many have expressed disdain towards political correctness[148]. It proves difficult for people to understand that political correctness is not some tacit system of code switching. Bodies of privilege are being pushed to be respectful of different marginalized communities to which they don't belong to and asked to recognize that speech they used and use has *always* been offensive and perpetuated oppression. Just because people are now being told that it is a problem, doesn't mean it hasn't always been a problem, because it has been. What is so phenomenal about this, is that privileged groups demand that they gain back power through freedom of speech, not realizing that free speech should not be an excuse for hateful discourse. To understand the distinction of free speech and hate speech is to understand that speech as a form of violence that encroaches on one's ability to equitably, equally, and safely navigate through society. However, many would rather switch terminology into something that positions them to be perceived as a suppressed people in relation to the expression of their rights. Many would rather minimize the impact they have on a community while arguing that the nation is in an era of heightened sensitivity.

When the marginalized resist, we are met with violence, criminalization, and the direct recognition that not much has changed at all. Stereotypes come flooding in rather than seeing what is right in front of our eyes. The poisonous fruit of our colonized minds continue to perceive resistance as anti-American. Resistance is seen as an unwillingness to be unified, while not realizing that asking marginalized groups to be united with the status quo determines and solidifies their fate in socio cultural, political, and economic destitution. When resistance is seen, we define this as civil disobedience, but why have we not reframed that terminology? In essence, how is disobedience in the face of blatant and implicit oppression not warranted? We infantilize and act paternalistically, taking agency away from a people by utilizing the word "disobedience". The way we frame resistance against marginalization consistently makes the system in place seem like the authority on body control. This extends directives to marginalized bodies on how to behave accordingly despite lives being destroyed by a system that claims their activities are un-American. What is un-American exactly? What inclusive unified front has this nation ever had where it does not

---

[148] Kumar, Deepa. "Race, ideology, and empire." *Dialectical Anthropology* 39, no. 1 (2015): 121.

demonize particular groups of people to gain support for its cause? Whatever it means to be American depends on your positionality. For those who have never been extended the rights and the options slated in direct terms of our Constitution, Bill of Rights, or Declaration of Independence - how can we even call ourselves American if we have seen that colonized America doesn't see or care about all of the bodies that inhabit this land? When there is no actualization of what it means to have human dignity, unalienable and natural rights, for abolishment to mean nothing more than the removal physical shackles for some and the retention of implicit shackles on many others. Americanism seems far from the dream that is purports itself to be the defender of.

Criminalization

Resistance has a direct correlation to incarceration and is also another form of violence we have set in place while claiming that the prison system was supposed to be one of restitution and rehabilitation[149]. It may be a form of rehabilitation for the privileged, but overall it is simply another privatized form of our economy that benefits the oligarchic aristocracy within our representative democracy. Prison and its industrial complex[150] sees resistance and autonomy as criminal, and rehabilitation has never been the main purpose of prisons. It has been for control of bodies especially the marginalized so that they can be "out of the way" of progress that the United States wants to make without them[151.] It does not account for how structured barriers made prison systems so proximal to marginalized communities. The prison system practices pure disposability, racial favoritism, offers disproportionate resources and assistance to marginalized bodies, and its presence and mechanisms do not work socially or in terms of recidivism[152]. In this, is

[149] Behan, Cormac. "Learning to escape: Prison education, rehabilitation and the potential for transformation." *Journal of Prison Education and Reentry* 1, no. 1 (2014): 20-31.
[150] Sudbury, Julia. *Global lockdown: Race, gender, and the prison-industrial complex.* Routledge, 2014.
[151] Earle, Chris S. "Dispossessed: Prisoner Response-Ability and Resistance at the Limits of Subjectivity." *Rhetoric Society Quarterly* 46, no. 1 (2016): 47-65.
[152] Mitchell, Ojmarrh, Joshua C. Cochran, Daniel P. Mears, and William D. Bales. "Examining Prison Effects on Recidivism: A Regression Discontinuity Approach." *Justice Quarterly* (2016): 1-26.

abolishment not a viable topic to give thought to in determining how to reconfigure community accountability that isn't driven by isms within a broken system?[153] Granted, there are conversations to be held on those who commit deplorable crimes that should pay restitution in some form. However, considering the disproportionate sentencing of the marginalized in comparison to the privileged- it's clear that justice is based on the perceptions we have of the marginalized[154]. Political resistance crimes are constantly met with disproportionate sentencing, as it is seen as a threat to the power those in place of power have. When we discuss violent crimes, we do have to talk about the nuance of it, especially when configuring alternatives to rehabilitative practices. It cannot be said that someone who is a victim of violence should have to know that the person that jeopardized their autonomy will not receive any form of punitive response. It's not in our socialization to be at that space of what forgiveness means, but it could be. Do we want punishment, constructive consequence or help and rehabilitation? Are they mutually exclusive? The question remains- can everyone be rehabilitated and what forms of restitution can make way for psychologically developing what forgiveness can be? And in what ways can we channel restitution into a form that restores or transforms our society's perception of crime and community accountability overall? However, when we discuss "restorative justice" for the criminal justice - we must eradicate that phrase from our rhetoric. We can't restore a system that has never at its foundation been a just practice and that was ultimately used to continue to marginalize historically marginalized bodies post-slavery[155]. We have to start over.

When one reenters society, if they managed to not get more time while in prison- what tools or resources are we extending to them to be functioning in society again? In what ways have we taken away their political power and demand that previously incarcerated people divulge their crimes? This practice reifies the sway from rehabilitation under the veil of false transparency and in the poli-

---

[153] Davis, Angela Y. *The meaning of freedom: And other difficult dialogues.* City Lights Books, 2013.

[154] Spohn, Cassia. "Racial disparities in prosecution, sentencing, and punishment." *The Oxford handbook of ethnicity, crime, and immigration* (2013): 166-193.

[155] Alexander, Michelle. *The new Jim Crow: Mass incarceration in the age of colorblindness.* The New Press, 2012.

cies that don't allow those with a felony to receive educational financial aid continues to control the trajectory of people. Marginalization continues to occur in policies that don't allow those with a felony to receive financial aid as well and in other policies that continue to control the trajectory of a people. We must adjust the way we practice justice.

We do realize the dysfunction in these governmental practices, yet we go along with them- the question left to answer is why? Maybe we fear giving up the minimal power that we have. As the land of the free that the United States touts itself to be, why do the people fear it more than they feel free within it? When we discuss precariousness, it is remiss to not talk about the notion of invisibility. When I use the term invisibility, I mean a different side of the same marginalizing coin. There is safety in invisibility, but there is also so much danger in it. With invisibility, it has been made clear that society has micro invalidated marginalized bodies and written their importance out of our narrative. However, this problem is emphasized when we erase ourselves to remain in some realm of safety[156]. How much safety can be in automating our own oppression within the system by erasing ourselves. There are ways that oppression operates that leaves many of us in "Catch 22" situations. If we're not seen or heard from, we're able to continue to navigate through barriers, but that doesn't make the barriers go away. When we resist and push back and make ourselves visible, we're a target and there is no safety in that. Though a certain amount of safety can, at times, be gained with a supportive and dedicated community.

One example concerning invisibility can be seen within the topic migration. It has been supposed that if migratory bodies don't make "waves", they may still be able to navigate in a system that labels their bodies as "illegal". When students began to uplift and state that they were undocumented, there was a strong sense of fear but also empowerment in those actions[157]. What came of decreasing this invisibility was that this generation has made it clear that they recognize these barriers won't go away. If we don't say something now

---

[156] Merryfield, Merry M. "Why aren't teachers being prepared to teach for diversity, equity, and global interconnectedness? A study of lived experiences in the making of multicultural and global educators." *Teaching and teacher education* 16, no. 4 (2000): 429-443.

[157] Nicholls, Walter. *The DREAMers: How the undocumented youth movement transformed the immigrant rights debate.* Stanford University Press, 2013.

- life won't ever change, it won't ever get better. Though migratory bodies used their strength to catalyze self empowerment, refusing to be invisibilized placed them in peril of deportation, but to many resistance is pivotal to shift the narrative and demand respect for their lives. This is not going to be everyone's story, but this is one way to process the need for change and the bubbling over of the mess and destruction that colonization has made. This alternative fruit of the mind are the seeds that we need rather than the same ones that we have continued to plant intergenerationally in the past.

Black bodies have never been able to live invisibly, but have more over existed with the hypervisibility and expectation of stereotypes and stigmas in ways that approve mistreatment by the general public. As increased brutality and disposability continues[158]. Resistance was seen as a necessary action. There was a need to those within power and privilege understand that the civil rights era wasn't enough progress. It has come to a point that as collective, black and brown bodies have agreed that the lives we are living, the limited trajectory we have, and the minimal years of our mortality inform the urgency of resisting injustice. In this, we decrease whatever invisibility we have because we would rather sacrifice our bodies for our own autonomy than to be continue to be oppressed.

When we discuss Native invisibility, it is a harrowing conversation to have because we have taken lives and taken land. We constantly glorify colonization and leave paragraphs at a time in textbooks to discuss the nation's accountability in the attempted destruction of a people with minimal accounts and limited representation[159]. Now as Native and indigenous populations continue to fight for land that rightfully belongs to them, to do with what they will, we see that a rise from being invisible was necessary. This rise was necessary because their sovereignty is once again being threatened and taken away. This rise was necessary because their culture continues to be appropriated and profited from.[160]. This nation makes marginalized bodies invisible far too easily and Native populations don't deserve

---

[158] Garza, Alicia. "A herstory of the# blacklivesmatter movement." (2014).

[159] Leavitt, Peter A., Rebecca Covarrubias, Yvonne A. Perez, and Stephanie A. Fryberg. ""Frozen in Time": The Impact of Native American Media Representations on Identity and Self-Understanding." *Journal of Social Issues* 71, no. 1 (2015): 39-53.

[160] Berry, Wendell. *The unsettling of America: Culture & agriculture.* Counterpoint, 2015.

to continue to be crushed under the weight of the nation's retained manifest destiny approach to upward mobility. If we remain hyper-visible and marginalized or invisibilized, we will perish anyway. If not in body, then in spirit.

When we discuss queer populations with all the intersections we may hold, there has always been a sense of safety in invisibility, in passing[161]. How much freedom exist in being suppressed and stifled, in being told that any hegemonic transgression will be met with stripping of rights and violence. What kind of system can take away rights from people so easily based on their private and con-sensual lives? To be able to take away someone's livelihood, to con-flate sexual deviancy into one category without understanding that it's not deviant or un-American is something that queer populations have been fighting forever. We demonize people globally for their violence towards LGBTQQIA2S+ populations. Yet, we kill the spirit of those within the nation state while seeing their lives as less than when tales of violence towards queer bodies are barely made visi-ble[162]. We have criminalized these bodies for so long that being invisible or passing became a standard way of life in public space. If that be the case, public space has never been for the full public and the marginalized continue to be seen as less deserving body con-cerning safety within it. Again, resistance comes to the fore because at this point- what is there to lose if living in invisibility kills our spirits, our souls, and oppresses the possibilities of fruitful existen-tialism? Those who are not in the queer population continue to rationalize the theft of the queer population's autonomy without interruption in masses, as the United States continues to develop policies that protect the privileged and those in power so that they continue to disenfranchise and infringe upon the rights of a people.

It's very clear that our bodies aren't perceived to matter equitably or even equally. We may be a diverse population, and we use it as a tagline. However, we do not treat each other with the same respect nor do we extend the same levels of freedoms or rights to everyone. This dynamic is so complex because invisibility of the power that makes this structural dysfunction continue is difficult to conti-

---

[161] Smith, Valerie. *Not just race, not just gender: Black feminist readings.* Routledge, 2013.

[162] Lind, Amy. ""Out" in International Relations: Why Queer Visibility Mat-ters." *International Studies Review* 16, no. 4 (2014): 601-604.

nuously call out in the face of policies that protect itself in the superficial attempt to try to make our society "better".

While some may be able to pass, others cannot. When we talk about disabilities, we have to understand the distinction between visible and invisible ones and know that those that can be invisible can shift to visible. When we discuss physical disabilities, the ability to be invisible is again, not a simple feat and is done so in trying to not take up space as if we aren't deserving of space all the same. When ADA was set in policy many complained about the economic burden it would take knowing that they never had to "deal" with these accommodations. The acceptance of these statements was so common because of the past asylum institutionalization practices. The public refused to push itself to understand the lack of humanity that was rampant in those institutions[163]. This lack of humanity encompassed forced invisibilization, body control, and disposability. Instead of seeing people, they saw economics. When we discuss invisible disabilities, this is when we realize how much the United States hinges on markers of quickly identify what's "wrong" with a person, that person can be subjugated to the invalidation of expressed needs. When your disability is invisible, you become even more so erased from the narrative. As people with varying abilities are being more clear about their needs, they in this, are pushing back on this notion of what disability "looks" and feels like[164].

Hetero Patriarchal White Supremacist Practices

The colonized nation state of the United States hinges every part of operation from the micro to the macro level, on heteropatriarchal white supremacist foundation. Our society demands adherence to uniformity under the guides and guidance of historical oppression that favors white, male, able bodied bodies above anything else[165]. The practices may seem explicit in some crevice of our society, but boldly implicit in others. From our race, gender, sexuality, nation of origin to our ability- there are expectations to how a body should

---

[163] Baynton, Douglas C. "Disability and the justification of inequality in American history." *The disability studies reader* 17 (2013): 33-57.

[164] Arvin, Maile, Eve Tuck, and Angie Morrill. "Decolonizing feminism: Challenging connections between settler colonialism and heteropatriarchy." *Feminist Formations* 25, no. 1 (2013): 8-34.

[165] Valdes, Francisco. "Unpacking hetero-patriarchy: tracing the conflation of sex, gender & (and) sexual orientation to its origins." *Yale JL & Human.* 8 (1996): 161.

present itself within public space. In a heteropatriarchal white supremacist society- race is consistently marginalized along with genders beyond male. We operate on a binary in most of everything we do. Again, when we revisit the "us vs. them" narrative, it becomes astoundingly transparent that the different ways that this supremacist approach has been implemented instructs the ways in which we can live our lives.

When we create a hierarchy of bodies, wherein no marginalized body can achieve the mobility possible for those in power, social mobility and navigability in society becomes inundated with hurdles for the marginalized. Heteropatriarchal white supremacy demands an idea of compulsory normalcy. This normalcy expects parallels to eurocentrism and western sociopolitical dynamics that inform body value and body movement.

Compulsory normalcy posits that there is an expectation in the way that we behave, speak, appear, etc. We, by compulsion of rhetoric concerning what deviance and transgression are, expect everyone to be labeled as something without extending the autonomy for bodies to name themselves[166]. The coercively migrated were given the surnames of their slave-owners, being made to carry that burden through their lineage without knowing their own history. Those who come from Latinx backgrounds are pushed into selecting one surname rather than carrying out the tradition of carrying all of their ancestor's names and heritages with them. Assimilation and acculturation is one the greatest forms of coercive normalcy that leads to compulsive expectations. Native and Indigenous people were taken away from their homes and placed in schools that forced acculturation to align more to eurocentrism. People with varying abilities were taken out of society if money was available so that the society could operate as if they were never there. Society continues this expectation of what normal functioning people in society should look like[167]. We have had tensions arise from the most simple of transgressions with long or facial hair during the sixties[168]. The residual impact of these compulsory normal-

---

[166] Leary, Mark R., and June Price Tangney, eds. *Handbook of self and identity.* Guilford Press, 2011.

[167] Adams, David Wallace. *Education for Extinction: American Indians and the Boarding School Experience, 1875-1928.* University Press of Kansas, 2501 W. 15th St., Lawrence, KS 66049, 1995.

[168] McAdam, Doug. "Culture and social movements." In *Culture and Politics,* pp. 253-268. Palgrave Macmillan US, 2000.

cy expectations is that it gained notoriety in fields that holds heavy influences on our livelihoods- positions, jobs, especially ones with power[169]. The caveat to all of this is that marginalized bodies are and continue to be seen as less than. There is however, a requirement of denouncing one's own culture and aligning to eurocentrism at the detriment of one's own self efficacy. We again bear strange fruit that lead to our down fall with minimal other options- seeing that commerce has been curtained off for the marginalized in many ways as earlier discussed. Freedom often has a price, and everyone doesn't feel like they can afford it when positionality puts food on the table.

Marginalized bodies have continued to operate on planes of double, triple, quadruple consciousness, and implement impression management based on their intersections. Marginalized populations change the way we speak, the way our hair appears, our dialect, our names, learn how to deal with invasive questioning and prodding all because we need a job, housing, or we need to be seen as docile and not criminal[170]. We adjust our gender expression, the kinds of conversations we have in public space. This expectation of normalcy destroys people a generation at a time as each preceding generation that has been marginalized, socializes their offspring to make these circumstances work to move forward; to be safe[171]. However, have we moved forward? We consistently expect everyone to be heterosexual to be heterosexual until proven otherwise and many "you're one of the good ones" when the privileged speak about people of color if they ostensibly accommodate the notion of normalcy to survive. We normalize brutality placed on a people if they do not align to expectations of heteropatriarchal white supremacy or just because they exist." Many epistemology slates were wiped clean for marginalized people. Colonialism made it impossible for many cultures to retain a full historical way of being. It has to be understood. It has to be understood that this is not one concept to graze over. It has destroyed people's lives and ability to live in a

---

[169] Harris, Fredrick C. "The rise of respectability politics." *Dissent* 61, no. 1 (2014): 33-37.

[170] Mullen, Harryette. "Optic white: blackness and the production of whiteness." *diacritics* 24, no. 2/3 (1994): 71-89.

[171] Hughes, Diane, James Rodriguez, Emilie P. Smith, Deborah J. Johnson, Howard C. Stevenson, and Paul Spicer. "Parents' ethnic-racial socialization practices: a review of research and directions for future study." *Developmental psychology* 42, no. 5 (2006): 747.

dignified way. Colonialism tells the marginalized that their body, who they are, that their culture, their being is not good enough to be present or have value within our society unless you are spectacle or being consumed while simultaneously being disposed of.

Marginalized groups have found ways to exist despite these normalcy expectations in their private lives, but that too can be invaded or destroyed because again it does not align to eurocentrism-in food, in music, in art, an in the ability for marginalized populations to exist freely together[172]. The expectation of compulsory normalcy robs a people of freedom in the most fundamental way. Not aligning to normalcy has gotten people killed, made people sacrifice their autonomy, and made people feel that their safety in continuously in peril. White supremacy implemented this heteropatriarchal function of our society and never sought to unravel it or acknowledge that it is still being used in criminalization and punishment, in education , in where one can live, and in what jobs we can achieve[173]. Every transgression from the heteropatriarchal white supremacist expectation is conflated with an invalid stereotype perpetuated by the emphasized superiority of whiteness.

When we discuss whose body matters and we look at what has taken place in the United States for the last 300 years- one cannot refute who is perceived to matter and ho is disposable. Revisiting our first statement- yes everybody is supposed to matter- but white supremacy and heteropatriarchy has made it clear that the marginalized, without question, do not. With this detriment, we brutalize one another for being different. We recognize another for being different. Therefore, we must ask ourselves- different from what or who? Is it the difference one holds from those who oppress the marginalized and we are told to aspire to align to? When we try to align to those images and accept that we are marginal and not worth aspiring to be ourselves, we destroy the possibility of who we could become on our own accord. Understanding that we are different and that there is no "normal" , only hegemony, has to be significantly uplifted if we want to break this cycle that we have been burdened by. With the expectation of an idea of normalcy that isn't real- we all are falling and failing our community, our society, and ourselves. What is this for? It's a

---

[172] Earley, P. Christopher. "Self or group? Cultural effects of training on self-efficacy and performance." *Administrative Science Quarterly* (1994): 89-117.

[173] Smith, Andrea. "Indigeneity, settler colonialism, white supremacy." *Racial formation in the twenty-first century* (2012): 66-90.

question that no one can truly have an answer to, beyond retaining power and subjugating people to continued oppression. The notion of normalcy shows up in our media, in our schools in our professions- - and our society is broken in and continues to poison us all because of its pushed presence and expectation of adherence.

Chapter 3

What It Is and What It Ain't:
Public Space, Policy, and Practice

Who has full autonomy and access in public spaces that are and
have been deliberately controlled by the powerful and the privileged?

Urban Blight

When we discuss urban blight it must be understood that the blight
that befell urban spaces was a direct consequence of sheer and
utter neglect. After World War II, the United States made clear that it
wanted to remodel how society operates and how it is viewed internally as well as externally[174]. When the United States incentivized
the suburbs, it failed to extend similar resources to the marginalized
and disenfranchised population[175]. In essence, the United States
allowed urban spaces to reach decay. The words "urban space" or
"inner city" quickly became stigmatized and the worth of space
quickly became connected to the bodies who inhabited the area. So
when we hear words like "inner city" or "urban", we know through
dog whistle politics, that they mean low income people of color[176].
They are disadvantaged and marginalized because the government
set that process in place. The government and society blamed the
people of those areas for the area's state approved systemic neglect.
When others decided that they wanted to live closer to the city center, the municipalities, independent contractors, and developers
worked in collusion to displace people who have lived in these urban areas through generations were pushed out of the plans of

---

[174] Kellner, Douglas. Media culture: Cultural studies, identity and politics
between the modern and the post-modern. Routledge, 2003.

[175] Feagin, Joe R. The new urban paradigm: Critical perspectives on the city.
Rowman & Littlefield, 1998.

[176] Haney-López, Ian. Dog whistle politics: How coded racial appeals have
reinvented racism and wrecked the middle class. Oxford University
Press, 2015.

urban renewal and revitalization[177] as an attraction to the city and away from the suburbs grew and those who once resided within the cities core were pushed to its outskirts where resources were removed and followed the migratory patterns of hegemonic groups. In cyclical fashion, the government and society abandoned marginalized populations and when the government saw the opportunity to capitalize, they did. The work of the marginalized to create a community in any degree is deemed inconsequential and what they have is taken away. Now these areas are regulated, cleaned, and has consistent upkeep by the very same government that displaced communities of color, blamed them for its condition, and refused to give any resources similar to the ones had now, then.

Gentrification

With this urban renewal and revitalization came the growth of gentrification, wherein the most privileged bodies made a social contract with local governments to displace low income people of color neglected for 20 + years. Cities allowed for raised rents so exorbitantly high that residents had no choice but to move out of their homes with the narrative of making the city more attractive, when its blight was its own doing[178]. Many consider gentrification to be an issue where in low income and people of color are displaced, but truly it goes much deeper than that. Gentrification makes sure that those displaced can never return and a stigma of unsuitable residents is attached to their bodies, and that property values increase with the social capital of white residents[179]. Within the queer community, to make the private lives private and incentivize whiteness to come back into the city center the concept of homonormativity arose[180]. Consumerism became extremely powerful where if queer bodies aligned and abided by their prescribed gender roles and left their affection at the door of their homes they would be accepted with the additional expectation of being higher income consumer-

[177] Haymes, Stephen Nathan. Race, culture, and the city: A pedagogy for Black urban struggle. SUNY Press, 1995.

[178] Clark, Kenneth B. Dark ghetto: Dilemmas of social power. Wesleyan University Press, 1989.

[179] Palen, J. John, and Bruce London, eds. Gentrification, displacement, and neighborhood revitalization. SUNY Press, 1984.

[180] Duggan, Lisa. "The new homonormativity: The sexual politics of neoliberalism." Materializing democracy: Toward a revitalized cultural politics (2002): 175-94.

ists in the area, they ignore displacement and embrace neoliberalism[181]. As gentrification grew it became even more clear that there was a substantial price tag on homes that were once seen as blighted- the cities immersed more funding in its revitalization. One prominent component of this practice being that those who are deemed undesirable were kept out of the very neighborhoods that they were forced to live in due to post World War II segregation tactics. Now, at present day, urban renewal based gentrification has left many without familial homes and sent the marginalized to the outskirts of urban hubs with lesser healthcare, food options, increased environmental precarity, and minimal transportation on which they depend[182]. The Young unmarried professionals with disposable income (yuppie) and the Not In My Backyard (NIMBY)[183] protocols set forth in neighborhoods set forth have made it nearly impossible and implausible for low income people of color to live in the urban areas they once dwelled. The marginalized population's social, cultural and economic capital seen as not enough to pay the entry fee in an area they once called their own. The marginalized were also faced with the realization that investment in property was more important than investing in the people of a community that has been marginalized by the government continuously. As business and municipalities invest in the area's growth in ways that would be unconscionable for the marginalized, cities extended these options to those who have privileged resources without pause. Now, will cities invest in building marginalized communities in such a substantial way to similar heights?

Gentrification did not only displace people, it demonized and displaced culture and counterculture. Even with pink washing[184] and consumerism- where people of color congregate, the tradeoff is in the acceptance of being a spectacle as a dorm of acceptance of their bodies. Gentrification has done more damage to marginalized communities than we care to admit. As the privileged pay for $20-

---

[181] Miller, Toby. Cultural citizenship: Cosmopolitanism, consumerism, and television in a neoliberal age. Temple University Press, 2007.

[182] Palen, J. John, and Bruce London, eds. Gentrification, displacement, and neighborhood revitalization. SUNY Press, 1984.

[183] Dear, Michael. "Understanding and overcoming the NIMBY syndrome." Journal of the American Planning Association 58, no. 3 (1992): 288-300.

[184] Lubitow, Amy, and Mia Davis. "Pastel injustice: The corporate use of pinkwashing for profit." Environmental Justice 4, no. 2 (2011): 139-144.

dollar cover fees to bars, cisgender people infiltrate once authentic and safe queer spaces to see people as things to be spectacled, co-opt culture, or display their cultural appropriation. It becomes clear that more than homes were lost. Communities of color were losing their ways of being, and in this, the various cultures that were the heartbeat of the city center was commodified[185]. The United States continuously tells people where they can and can't be. One's gender, gender expression, sexuality, color or ability all dictate how we are watched and regulated as "visitors". In this, we continue to lack self-agency. Even when economic currency is held, your body remains subject to surveillance based on the historical stereotypes that were present before one's birth.

Surveillance

Understanding that body control and body value as well as the boundary lines that the Western Imaginary draws the influence on criminalization must be discussed. Stereotypes among different groups shift within the social atmosphere of the United States. With "freedom" given and not rightfully had outright with marginalized population, what has become another piece of strange fruit from the tree of colonization has been the compulsion to surveil those that have been conditionally freed.

After slavery and after the suffrage movement, the passage of ADA, the queer liberation movement and the different wave of feminism along with the temporary protections of Deferred Action of Childhood Arrivals (DACA) and Deferred Actions of Parents of Americans (DAPA), we have consequentially fell victim to pervasive forms of surveillance. This surveillance is protected under the narrative of the nation's best interest even when what it propagandized itself to be is at the detriment of marginalized people[186]. DACA and DAPA have been used to tout temporary freedoms for undocumented persons, but in actuality registering for the program allows them to be surveilled at any time the government feels the need or whimsy to do as such.

---

[185] Bunten, Alexis Celeste. "Sharing culture or selling out? Developing the commodified persona in the heritage industry." American Ethnologist 35, no. 3 (2008): 380-395.
[186] Fernandez, Luis A., and Laura Huey. "Is resistance futile? Thoughts on resisting surveillance." Surveillance & Society 6, no. 3 (2009): 199-202.

Post 9/11 we began to surveillance people under the suspicion of terrorism in ways that aided the government in surveilling all those who critiqued the United States practices.[187] What is so interesting about surveillance, is that those with power and privilege are rarely besieged by this imposition. After 9/11, black and brown bodies began to be surveilled and harassed at a significantly higher rate and at a visibly higher rate that the government and the general public approved of[188]. To be a person of color continues to be a crime in the United States at an expedited rate with blatant disregard to natural and inalienable rights governmentally and socially.

We must also have more conversations discussing how surveillance fails to observe or use language apropos to white domestic terrorism in hate crimes. The bodies assumed to be affiliated with these crimes perpetuate the notion that the privileged do not align with crimes that would be considered as unpatriotic or an attempt or create mass terror by perpetuation of -isms. In this lack of policy applicability for the privileged, the government commits treason upon itself. There have been many approaches taken to surveil from Cointelpro to the Patriot Act to Stop and Frisk[189]- some things are mentioned explicitly, and some other practices are redacted from public record.[190] Due to national security we often use this terminology to operate as authoritative vigilantes. Some forms of violence that have come of surveillance are never answered for and the way that we surveil is constantly excused without acknowledgement of wrongdoing or a response to community members that are affected by it. Through enforcing disproportionate surveillance we directly impact the safety of those we watch commonly without cause because public knowledge of surveillance has structural and social ramifications in regards to actions, perceptions, and their

---

[187] Saito, Natsu Taylor. "Whose Liberty-Whose Security-The USA PATRIOT Act in the Context of COINTELPRO and the Unlawful Repression of Political Dissent." Or. L. Rev. 81 (2002): 1051.

[188] Webb, Maureen. Illusions of security: Global surveillance and democracy in the post-9/11 world. City Lights Books, 2007.

[189] Saito, Natsu Taylor. "Whose Liberty-Whose Security-The USA PATRIOT Act in the Context of COINTELPRO and the Unlawful Repression of Political Dissent." Or. L. Rev. 81 (2002): 1051.

[190] Cole, David, and James X. Dempsey. Terrorism and the constitution: Sacrificing civil liberties in the name of national security. The New Press, 2006.

byproducts of discrimination forms from government agencies to public citizens by influence.

Nuances of Citizenship: De Jure, De Facto, and Assimilation

When we discuss citizenship, we must do so with a lens that shows its ability to sparse out nuances. Citizenship in a sense is very real, with very real implications. On the other hand, we have to reflect upon citizenship from a Western framework. How is it that colonists who took over land, took it upon themselves to be the gatekeepers to who can enter, who can exit and who is deemed an actual citizen? It seems preposterous that those who immigrated to the United States and committed mass genocide and atrocities of slavery can be in any position to delegate what we call citizenship. In recent works, many have used terms such as racial citizenship and sexual citizenship[191]. I feel that these terms with various preceding identifiers exemplify that due to marginalization, that full citizenship is true but marginalized populations are hyperaware that it is not.

How can we consider ourselves citizens under a regime of oppression where every entrance fee is based on the economic, symbolic, and social capital that we hold?

As we condition the population to understand immigration, we must explore how citizenship has existed on a plane of duality in dichotomous sectors of the "haves" and "have nots". Those "having" being ones in power due to heteropatriarchal white supremacy, and the "have nots" being those impacted by supremacist practices. We look at citizenship within the United States as something sacred, but in truth. For the marginalized they have de jure wording with de facto paradox. If we look at slavery- blacks were considered three fifths of a person[192]. They had no voting rights and their population was only counted to maintain the status quo of the slavery that took their autonomy away from them. If we look at Native and indigenous populations, they have been murdered and stripped of their land. The only time the United States government saw fit to deem them American citizenship was so they could be indoctrinated, assimilated, and acculturated to the formalization of what we refer

---

[191] Evans, David. Sexual citizenship: The material construction of sexualities. Routledge, 2013.

[192] Ohline, Howard A. "Republicanism and slavery: origins of the three-fifths clause in the United States Constitution." The William and Mary Quarterly: A Magazine of Early American History (1971): 563-584.

to as American culture. This culture is one of white supremacy with pronounced subordination of marginalized populations. The United States also sought to make Native American citizens to rule over their sovereignty with federal United States laws and regulation that sought to further dispossess a people.

When looking at those with disabilities, it becomes again harrowingly clear that their citizenship was never negotiable and as they were seen to also be undesirable, there was no autonomy[193]. We stripped these marginalized populations from their citizenship by controlling their bodies, marginalizing them, and throwing them into institutions that sought their demise. Not once did hegemony realize that we all are different and that nothing is wrong with a body, but moreover, that the world is only built structurally and spatially to cater to particular types of people that hold power and influence.

Once slavery was outlawed we are familiar with how criminalization tactics towards nonwhite bodies have been affected by de jure and de facto distinctions of citizenship. How can one be considered a full citizen if the Declaration of Independence and the Bill of Rights are not applicable to some and if policies are set forth to control or criminalize their autonomy[194]. What is evident is the manners by which we have implicitly set forth state of mind wherein we devalue bodies of color and other intersectional marginalizations in the practices of our society despite de jure policies.

When we discuss sexual citizenship and gender variance, it too becomes clear that if assimilation and passing is not an option taken, then safety in citizenship status is not held either. Much of the degree of citizenship that we are extended is contingent upon capital . Ultimately, varying from the normalcy narrative gives way to precarity and conditional citizenship above anything else. What can be taken away from the notion of sexual citizenship is that it has been made quite clear that Congress, States, and politicians are the bodies that hold control over one's body and one's ability to function in consensual households the way they choose. Anti-

---

[193] Ware, Norma C., Kim Hopper, Toni Tugenberg, Barbara Dickey, and Daniel Fisher. "Connectedness and citizenship: Redefining social integration." Psychiatric Services 58, no. 4 (2007): 469-474.

[194] Woodward, Comer Vann. The strange career of Jim Crow. Oxford University Press, USA, 1955.

discrimination policies have been set in place, but the minimal amount to which they are implemented is disparaging[195].

The public display of affection alone or ownership over one's body despite body size, looks, gender, or orientation is constantly met with dynamic shifts that find ways to align to oppression. How can full citizenship be held when a woman cannot walk down the street without being harassed, when masculine entitlement bends its will to those who barricade autonomy of choice? How can citizenship be had when reproductive decisions are controlled by a governmental faction in ways that continue to see bodily autonomy as a salient issue? We can expand this conversation to documentation, sexuality, gender and gender identity, race, and ability. The bottom line is that marginalized populations have been made to answer to the government and figure out the safest way to live their lives with that understood power dynamic.

What we as marginalized folks have to take care in is to not reproduce the same fruit of this continued marginalization or align to the nuanced definitions of citizenships just to give ourselves minimal ideas of power over the ones we oppress. Citizenship is again a construct and its flux in definition continues to behoove those in power, to allow its nuance to remain in place. The issue with policies that grant or deny citizenship is that they make it difficult to argue that equality has not come to fruition, it makes it difficult to explain to people that what we have amended has not amended any of the wounds the marginalized have and still suffer. It's not that the policies aren't worded eloquently- it is that there is minimal oversight for infraction of them towards the marginalized and it is that the implementation of its surface based purpose is continuously carried out in a mediocre way. This saves those who stand by policies as an instrument of past amelioration for nefarious behavior from doing the hard work of truly implementing equitable policy. The ability to rationalize the articulation of continued oppression as a sense of paranoia of the marginalized, it relied upon dismissal to continue to stoke the fire of oppression based behavior. Policies also seek to immediately absolve guilty parties as if one

---

[195] Crenshaw, Kimberle Williams. "Race, reform, and retrenchment: Transformation and legitimation in antidiscrimination law." Harvard Law Review (1988): 1331-1387.

policy for centuries of tragedy are that easy to eradicate from its residual impacts listed in the previous chapters[196].

On the judicial level, it is clear that there is disproportionality of treatment among the privileged and the marginalized, but people see what they want to see and the optics by which we see the world is contingent on the lives of privilege or oppression we have experienced. Often privileged groups hinge on some identifier or qualifier to conflate the ideas of oppression, such as poverty, to be resulting failure of the individual. We know that poverty for a white able bodied person and poverty for an undocumented, racial minority, woman of color, or a person of limited ability is far more difficult to rise above because of the system by which we live in[197]. We know, that we as a society continue to treat people differently due to stereotypes and stigmas placed on bodies that those with capital never have to face. In finding some way to conflate the momentary experiences of misfortune as marginalization for the privileged, the privileged reduce the experience of the marginalized by demanding that they, too, understand the strife of limited or absent citizenship as well as policy. There's absolutely no way that they could compare these experiences. Groups that don't want to acknowledge oppression find a way to bring the frame to themselves and their imaginary plight that is not structural..

Bureaucratic Implementation Breakdown

Unjust policies have been deemed permissible and are present today as unjust as they were in the past in various ways. We also have de jure policies that tout and ostensibly promote equality rather than equity or justice that has never come societally to fruition in a de facto sense.

In the previous section I discuss how policies and governing bodies dictate the ways we live our lives after they are elected by the majority and how we fail to acknowledge fundamental non-negotiable rights. These rights include body autonomy, sovereignty, and safety. We also must take a look at how these policies, de jure or de facto, breakdown within organizational governing and non-

---

[196] Macias, Reynaldo F. "Inheriting sins while seeking absolution: Language diversity and national statistical data sets." DOCUMENT RESUME (1994): 23.

[197] Quadagno, Jill S. The color of welfare: How racism undermined the war on poverty. Oxford University Press, 1994.

governmental bodies at the will or neglect of those who work within their systems.

Despite any argument that may come, we are human beings that work within our own specializations within society. We all have some part in the way it functions and what we socially deem as acceptable and ignorable. We have to take a look at the historical lack of access the marginalized have had in these positions and how that continues on in ways that are apparent in the demographics of many functioning bodies of society. Marginalized bodies have consistently been allowed access to what society deems to be harmless and menial positions[198]. As social mobility in increments became possible, the threat felt by those in power, that they may have to share power and found other tactics to thwart the access of the marginalized. We must share power, whether it is in hiring practices, in deconstructing how we see white supremacy as the "look of professionalism", and address sexual harassment and targeting[199]. It became apparent when affirmative action benefited white women over any other demographic and not people of color with varying abilities. This was an enacted strategy to superficially adhere to policies in a way that people who wish to resist diversity and inclusion, can in a way that seems as if they are ameliorating for discriminatory practices[200]. That's not a coincidence- it is circumvention and aligning to as well as scaffolding the capital of different bodies with different intersectional distinctions.

We as human beings are capable of being rational, but the issue lies within what we decide to rationalize. If our minds have been colonized to refer back to stereotypes and stigmas, we rationalize the perpetuation of oppression. We fail to allow access to systems where the marginalized could have social mobility and a heightened self-advocacy. We must understanding and interrupting oversight (not that that is the responsibility of all marginalized people). Furthermore, there have been several moments when equality based policies and initiatives have been set forth. However, just because they are created and set forth does not mean they are

[198] Van Dijk, Teun A. "Discourse, power and access." Texts and practices: Readings in critical discourse analysis (1996): 84-104.
[199] Aggarwal, Arjun P., and M. Gupta. "Sexual harassment in the workplace." Editorial Board (2000): 16.
[200] Katznelson, Ira. When affirmative action was white: An untold history of racial inequality in twentieth-century America. WW Norton & Company, 2005.

equitably implemented. We as human being within the United States context have been socialized to think and operate in an individualistic neoliberal way and a collective way when it benefits groups of power.

Marginalized groups understand how to share power because they've always had to, but that's not to say that there are not some marginalized that align themselves to heteropatriarchal white supremacist practices to individualistically get ahead by neoliberal strategy[201]. Nevertheless, policies without oversight become useless. Oversight is seen as a burden. Without oversight, there's no way to ensure that equitable policies are being carried out. In the past, and at present, there has been great resistance to equitable policies[202]. Without federal decree or force, it's unlikely that these policies would have ever been implemented albeit though many were substantially delayed. We underestimate the usefulness of oversight, the human condition to retain power, and the undeniable existence of oppressive practices within the psyche of those who function with society. It's not just superficial policy that is the problem- overall its implementation and a lack of a culture shift that gets people to understand that sharing power is the only step forward in a more equitable society. However, with our own biases towards oppression, we continue to live in ways that benefit hegemonic groups. There's a lack of accountability and reprimanding practices for those who barely practice or implement policies of equity, diversity, or inclusion. Or maybe, the intention was again to, in theory, offer a policy solution knowing that those in power would never allow it to happen. The system we live in wholeheartedly understands the spheres of influence that affect and impact the marginalized as well as the privileged. The system depends on these marginalizing impacts and autonomously carry out the intentions of colonial practices that keep the marginalized stifled from full citizenship and mobility within society.

---

[201] Kymlicka, Will. "Neoliberal multiculturalism." Social resilience in the neoliberal era (2013): 99-125.

[202] Shapiro, Sidney A. "Political Oversight and the Deterioration of Regulatory Policy." Administrative Law Review (1994): 1-40.

Chapter 4

The Institutions of Influence:
Education and the Media

We talked a bit before about spheres of influence throughout the preceding chapters. However, we need to invest further into exploring the institutions that dictate the way our society is introduced to, processes, and digests information. The way we encode and decode information is informed by the environmental microcosms. These microcosms consist of our own Venn diagrammatic interconnected communities, the dynamics therein, and the way we critically process transmitted information in an introspective and constructive manner. Two of the most influential institutions in our society to date that have the ability to disseminate information are education and media. From these institutions, we delve deeper into how the mechanisms of biolegitmacy[203] extend from theory to socio-political practice.

In the *Talented Tenth*, W.E.B Dubois states that "A university is a human invention for the transmission of knowledge and culture from generation to generation, through the training of quick minds and pure hearts"[204]. Though the Dubois' quote speaks from the context of post-secondary education, the idea of knowledge transmission rings true for all formal and informal models of education. This is true if epistemology is not destroyed, but valued and strengthened. However, our socialization, through various stages of development, has already begun to engrain itself into our ontology. This ingraining process is seen in the way that we see the world, make meaning from the different contexts we find our bodies within, and in the way we see ourselves. The expectation that we all are introduced to education in a space whose purpose is to transmit knowledge with an a priori of pure *anything* is presumptuous at

---

[203] Lemke, Thomas, Monica J. Casper, and Lisa Jean Moore. Biopolitics: An advanced introduction. NYU Press, 2011.
[204] Du Bois, William Edward Burghardt. *The talented tenth*. James Pott and Company, 1903.

best. Society impacts the ways we digest information and act accordingly from the meaning we've assigned to particular social dynamics happens far before we enter a school. Another pivotal set of questions that arises are: Who writes the syllabus? Who sets the goals? Who constructs the rubrics of learning? Who decides on the cannon of information or knowledge extended within those walls of a school? And if it is not an inclusive and informed collective, then how is it that we determine if they hold the competencies to make these decisions that dictate such an integral part of our lives. It is understood that by the time one, who has the ability to do so, reaches college – educators hold academic freedom[205]. Through primary and secondary school, educators are instructed to follow fine lines of what should be taught to ensure their safety in job security and the matriculation of their pupils. It is equally problematic that professors have the ability to exercise academic freedom in a way that continues to indoctrinate students to their biases that align to oppressive navigation through life rather than intellectual inquiry. What do we deem pertinent and what do we deem inconsequential? How is Aristotle more important than Frantz Fanon? How is pre-calculus more important than fiscal literacy in a capitalistic society where stocks rule our sustenance based security? Why is it that we don't constructively piece together the usefulness of geometry with architecture? Why do we value the term architecture more than carpentry? Why is it that, we learn ahistorical Western European History, but ethnic studies is never integrated in the overall scope of our collective historical epistemology? How are the wars we participated in, and the colonialized erasure based narrative of our negative participation, more important that the domestic terrorism we allow to persist due to white supremacy within our borders? The ways in which educational institutions have ruled out certain pieces of content of what goes into our educational funnel, sheds light on how it disenfranchises those without privilege. We leave minimal space for introspection, interruption and critical thought all the while creating a vast landscape for those who go through the steps of educational processes. Educational institutions depend more on recitation and neoliberalism than comprehension because that path leads to the mere *possibility* or social mobility. This creates decreased hope in the notion of gaining freedom

---

[205] Schrecker, Ellen. The lost soul of higher education: Corporatization, the assault on academic freedom, and the end of the American university. The New Press, 2010.

through education and heightens the cognizance of one's own sub-jugation to systemic manipulation.

Schools, in a traditional sense and as an educational institution, are at best a place of indoctrination, a filter, and its policies demand you be present on the conveyer belt. Not for your own wellbeing but for your utility in perpetuating a manufactured culture. What other institution demands your active participation through the three first stages of your psycho-social development?[206] The institution of education has a unique ability to mold minds and deem what "ap-propriateness" is. The power given to educational institutions also criminalize through truancy and behavior policies. These policies are pushed to be more applicable to marginalized communities, categorize value, socialize and reify social politics. The institution of education scaffolds the importance of particular occupations, and set barriers in place for social mobility access under the disguise of freedom. This disguise uses the philosophical idea of what educa-tion is *meant* to be rather than the *actuality* of what it really is- a systematic gate[207] .The educational system is more concerned with what one can contribute. These contributions are expected to feed into automated forms of structural demands for assimilation, the culture and capitulation, and control. This control exists under implicitly informed consent and institutional betrayal[208]. This be-trayal is interested in refusing to deconstruct its oppressive functio-nality. Institutional control ignores the possibility that we can learn from everything rather than a set scope of curriculum and that there is validity in other forms or components of knowledge trans-mission. Even though we did build curriculum with a scope- why is it that we do not transmit knowledge to ensure that we are capable of meeting our basic needs. Why have not ensured that we were able to function in the social and economic climate of where we live? How is it that, we don't teach agriculture, carpentry, and art in ways that are valued and more than an elective. Why are these aforementioned skills understood to be the work of the "less than" or seen as a simple spectacle for consumption? Is it that we are

---

[206] Greene, David. "Gatekeepers: the role of adult education practitioners and programs in social control." Journal for Critical Education Policy Studies 5, no. 2 (2007): 411-437.

[207] Fishel, Andrew, and Janice Pottker. "National Politics and Sex Discrimi-nation in Education." (1977).

[208] Smith, Carly Parnitzke, and Jennifer J. Freyd. "Institutional betrayal." American Psychologist 69, no. 6 (2014): 575.

advanced enough to not *have* to learn the importance and possibilities of these skills and forms of expression? Is this educational value
system mechanically in place to ensure that some people stay "in
their place"? By not being extended the opportunity to build on
educational competencies in ways that assist people in understanding how to function outside the parameters of the governmental and
economic systems we limit ourselves. With these limitations in place
we dilute the trajectory of our prosperity. In this, we also fail to have
the space to deconstruct the educational system that limits us.

   We have participated in a trend of excluding bodies from our educational system. We construct a narrative wherein it appears as if
access is granted. We behave as if the country is giving the marginalized a gift. This gift comes at a price of institutional perpetration of
historical marginalized dynamics. The access granted is undeniably
conditional with expectations of complying with implicit forms of
marginalization that align to the explicit policies seemingly de-
commissioned. Access to education is not necessarily a gift, and
should not be a tool of ensuring that generations adhere to a particular ontology, yet it is. You cannot pilfer rights from a people, give
them access to an institution after you have perfected it as a tool of
oppression and manipulation and then call it a gift. A "gift" that
demands compliance amongst the oppressed and creates such an
untouchable privileged class of a few that they rarely, if ever, have
the opportunity to see that something is disjointed. Disjointed, in
how they prevail in comparison to others in degrees that cannot be
explained away by meritocracy. The institution of education is designed in a way wherein we cannot see whose backs had to be broken in so that it's mobility and comfort (socially or politically) was
possible or more possible than most. The institution of education
continues to perfect its craft. With each body that is allowed or denied entry, we rationalize oppression with its evolving script in
pseudo legitimizing ways. These rationalizations are fed by social
stereotypes set in place that encourage people to participate in
complicity. To participate in looking for paradigms of behaviors
with marginalized communities to those stereotypes. This is done
so without the privileged questioning how their behaviors align to
these stereotypes that are given legitimacy for particular groups but
not for privileged groups at all. This practice is a contributing factor
to how we dehumanize and value one's legitimacy as a human being. This practice holds the marginalized to superhuman expectations while holding others to standards to which these same rubrics
are not applicable without explicit question or explanation. We

demand excellence within a system that limits a marginalized person's trajectory and demand adherence to its dynamics without question. All the while, others are extended the opportunity to express themselves freely and make human mistakes. This difference shows clear indications of disproportionality that we still fail to acknowledge. Disproportionalities that have impacted how policies are practiced within educational institutions and how behavior is rationalized or penalized depending on the social "markers" of one's body. A marginalized person's steps outside of adherence to a system solidifies expectation of their body value. But we only practice this with marginalized groups of people and fail to ever question why the same standards don't apply in institutions reaching far beyond just that of educational systems. We often assign different adjectives to similar actions and refuse to admit for whom specific words apply or explore by demographic trends of disproportionate applicability to an extent that we actually do anything to alter that outcome. The saying that "words will never hurt you" is simply untrue. Words perpetuate oppression in theory, throughout time, and within space without pause if no one interrupts their dynamics. We find ways to rationalize murder with created terms such as "affluenza"[209]. But we can't seem to rationalize the intergenerational impacts of lack of access for a marginalized person to break any level or categorization of a law. Specifying the ways we are, as a society, informed by the disproportionate treatment from a larger context is crucial. Emotional, behavioral, and mental healthcare for privileged bodies are topics spoken about in a humanizing manner. When these health issues are discussed concerning marginalized, they are met with disciplinary actions. These actions are ones of violence, control, or categorization that leads into special education placement. These actions are taken without exploring the root of the problem (if one is present) and working through it with a developing child. We have to stop saying we don't see marginalized bodies. If we pretend we can't see who someone is it makes it absolutely impossible to see the disparity you contribute to. Forced ignorance doesn't help anyone just because it makes you comfortable.

Access to formal education came with the expectation of mental and behavioral compliance for marginalized communities. Understanding that veering out of absolute compliance came with the

---

[209] MacMullan, Terrance. "Facing up to Ignorance and Privilege: Philosophy of Whiteness as Public Intellectualism." Philosophy Compass 10, no. 9 (2015): 646-660.

threat of falling into another institution; the criminal system. Being subjected to the criminal justice system or the oppressive dynamics of the institution of education ensured that the government had control regardless over a people's bodies. Through the practice of the "New Jim Crow"[210] and free prison/slave labor, the nation made clear that they would capitalize off of the body of the marginalized. This capitalization is pursued regardless of the institution the marginalized were a part of. The pipeline to the criminal justice system has always been fearfully palatable to those whose bodies have always been criminalized and disposed of[211]. This either/or practice of body filing exhibited the fixed value system and degrees of biolegitmacy we hold for the marginalized. There exist in a thin line between ostensible freedom within school systems and that of a school to prison pipeline that leads to an actual cage. This cage is one of stripped rights and minimal autonomy, being such a short stone's throw away from the intergenerational trauma of chains and dehumanization that never dissipated. This dynamic and inter-institutional relationship remained as a threat that this government has never paused to act on.

It's no surprise that the criminal and educational system work in partnership to ensure that it controls our society and who gets to function within it. These systems seek to break people in, to break them down, until they accept that all of their mind and body will never belong to them. This sense of belonging is unachievable unless one is willing to literally die to fight for the chance of self-authorship. This dynamic depletes access to resources to build one's self back up in a strategic way and continues to evolve towards the dissolution of our humanity's possibility.

Access based on documentation status, no matter how many individual institution policy amendments, still proves to be a federal problem regarding financial aid or unquestioned access to a higher education institution. Statements of equity and inclusivity don't matter if we don't act on them. Much like how test fee waivers for those of lower income, Pell grants and in-state tuition doesn't ameliorate the overall problem of testing or charging for it[212].

---

[210] Alexander, Michelle. "The New Jim Crow." Ohio St. J. Crim. L. 9 (2011): 7.

[211] Kim, Catherine Y., Daniel J. Losen, and Damon T. Hewitt. The school-to-prison pipeline: Structuring legal reform. NYU Press, 2010.

[212] McNeil, Linda. *Contradictions of school reform: Educational costs of standardized testing.* Routledge, 2002.

Educational institutions continue to develop standard practices that exclude. Most prominently beyond increasing tuition, identifying particular institutions to have more value or rank than others based on privilege. The economic and matriculation charge for standardized tests are of considerable concern as well. As if grades weren't enough, we demand students take and pay to be tested *again.* The Scholastic Aptitude Test (SAT), the American College Test (ACT) as well as graduation exams are all forms of getting out of one part of the educational system and getting placed into another. Paper is currency in money and in diplomas. Educational institutions claim that their schools are unique. If this is so, why have they not developed testing materials that go with the grain of what their institution expects rather than privatizing the entrance rubric? A rubric for educational access is designed under one common umbrella of the Educational Testing Service (ETS)? Why is there another standardized test at all? Why is the will to want to go to college not enough? Standardized tests overall have taken place of free thought and innovative curriculum. The tests have become a burden placed on caring educators, and the burden has also been placed on a generation to generation transmission of the unimportance of critical thought. I can't say that result wasn't the intention of these tests in the first place. The intention was to reinforce obedience, compliance, indoctrination and ranking of valued bodies. This tanking is reinforced through content and its demand to be an access checkpoint to matriculation and higher education.

We live in a society where the exclusion from education, the use of its presence as a place for acculturation, and its use as an environment. It is an environment that accepts where we filter degrees of worth among adolescents has been unquestionably present for marginalized communities. As intersectionality posits; race and other compounded marginalized identities alludes to the disenfranchisement of multiple dimensions of life and its quality. Intersectionality informs other institutions to dismiss one's body multiple times over. We fail to revisit the ways marginalization extends to social implications of exclusion or demanded acculturation. We need to explore how the practices of the educational institution inherently stifle the trajectory of demographics of people. Conservative or libertarian rhetoric often leans on the importance of neoliberalism and individualism. However, the validity of any argument falls flat if we acknowledge that *groups* of people are disenfranchised because of their identities. It rarely matters how hard one works if society has already dictated *who* you can be, *what* you have

access to, and *how* you have access to it. The "American Dream"
has fine print and doesn't take into account who has to suffer so
that the economically and socially "elite" can prevail and perpetuate its narrative. We behave as if chains are the only imagery of
slavery we can conceive and comprehend. We discuss freedom as if
we aren't steps away from being chained again based on the ways
that oppressive institutions are interconnected. We've sullied the
word freedom so much that we think its present when so many
policies are circumvented. This circumvention implies that marginalized bodies are not legitimate through faulty rationalization and
dog whistle politics[213]. This isn't freedom; we've just fooled ourselves into believing that it is in comparison to the past. On a fundamental level, we still haven't achieved freedom by any stretch of
the imagination. We've found some ways to navigate through oppression, but that doesn't mean we're free, and that doesn't mean
we should behave as if the state of being at present is comfortable
by any means. I fear double consciousness has given that impression. This isn't a new problem- it's *always* been a problem. But we
have to figure out how to survive so they can fight at other times. I
have no doubt that education can get us free. The education we
need just may not be held in the walls of a traditional school setting
that is a part of an institution that has always sought to control how
far someone can go and the limits of what they can learn. It's counterintuitive to its purpose to teach its deconstruction unless those
within its system operate subversively to survive in it and dismantle
its oppressive mechanisms. Mechanisms that seek to destroy us at
the same time with hopes of developing something better.

We continue to flash the image of strange fruit before the eyes of
youth and administrators in a way that it becomes normalized. This
normalization, continues as we cultivate and orchard of our own
demise. Oppression seeks to control the narrative and bodies. As
institutions concern themselves with caring about what was rationalized or accepted as "normal" without understanding the ills of
our culture that we have normalized. We have allowed the systemic
thorns to thrive in our educational institution and many other.
Who's holding the institutions accountable? Is that level of accountability even realistic?

---

[213] López, Ian Haney. Dog whistle politics: How coded racial appeals have
     reinvented racism and wrecked the middle class. Oxford University
     Press, 2015.

Public education has failed the marginalized but succeeded in what it intended to do after the industrial revolution. These identified successes revolved around keeping people in places that make this society comfortable and unthreatened. These are products of an institution that was and is averse to equitable power sharing. The Institution of education has always been one of the largest, structural, systemic, and cyclical weapons of mass destruction domestically used on its own population. I am not suggesting we privatize education because it needs to be a public service. However, I am absolutely suggesting that it needs to fully deconstruct its practice of how it operates at present. If that means a complete overhaul, so be it. Minimal changes in policies not adhered to is never going to eradicate injustice from a system. This is a system that took centuries to protect itself from a shift from its intended purpose. Maybe that means we need to teach our own communities what schools won't while navigating how to create something better. This construction would have to be something that revives the essence of the importance of education, knowledge and learning in an equitable and inclusionary sense. One thing is certain; the institution can't keep operating in this vein without eventually being completely privatized. If the educational system continues to perpetuate exclusion from quality education, it's set to implode. We need dismantling, we need interruptions, and we need new directions informed by an intersectional social justice lens. However, I am not sure if the system was not meant to self-destruct once inclusion and justice was demanded, giving way to the push for privatization that would again marginalized those who did not have capital to access equitable education.

Policies of Infringement and Social Perspective

It is impossible to extract the social context and perceptions from policies that impact the public education system. Through colonialism, Native American's were not only disenfranchised from the rightful sovereignty of their land but through educational processes in the late 1800's many within the indigenous population were coerced. These populations were coerced into boarding schools that demanded acculturation through demanding that their ways of being be erased being erased. Marginalized populations had their names replaced by Eurocentric ones and their language was sought to be devalued and destroyed[214]. Through this process, educational administrators used these boarding schools as a vehicle to destroy a culture and "reform" its pupils to contribute to the society that the country was attempting to mold. Measures of emotional, psychological, and sexual violence became prolific to dehumanize and break down a people to solely be present in society in ways deemed acceptable by those in power[215]. These violent practices of colonization extending from the body to the mind were a common practice for many marginalized populations. The African American population from as early as the era of slavery was also stripped of their culture, names, and ways of being as well[216]. In fact, there were several policies in place in the south that banned African Americans from being educated in any way that spread beyond slave labor. This practice attempted to destroy a people's epistemology. This practice also attempted to destroy a sense of historical self and barred their access to a formulated society on stolen land after being coercively migrated. This made their positionality within a society have a pre-defined scope that was meant to not to be altered. In this, we continue to dehumanize marginalized populations in manners that bar access to institutions intended for upward mobility. We influence body value perceptions for the general public to absorb through policy as well as social practice. This discrimination did not end there. As African Americans were granted segregated access to educational institutions, the narrative of their history was obfuscated from the curriculum. Educational resources were purposefully minimal in ways that impacted student's trajectory and ensured that the African American population could only go so far. Some cases such as *Plessy vs. Ferguson*[217] and *Brown vs. Board of Education*[218] challenged segregation. There remained

---

[214] Bernasconi, Robert. "On needing not to know and forgetting what one never knew: The epistemology of ignorance in Fanon's critique of Sartre." Sullivan and Tuana, Race and Epistemologies of Ignorance (2007): 231-38.

[215] Spring, Joel. Deculturalization and the struggle for equality: A brief history of the education of dominated cultures in the United States. Routledge, 2016.

[216] Fields, Barbara Jeanne. "Slavery, race and ideology in the United States of America." New Left Review 181 (1990): 95.

[217] Kousser, J. Morgan. "Plessy v. Ferguson." Dictionary of American History 6 (2003): 370-371.

[218] Bell Jr, Derrick A. "Brown v. Board of Education and the interest-convergence dilemma." Harvard Law Review (1980): 518-533.

pronounced resistance to social acceptance of policy change through multiple forms of violence making it clear just how well policy and practices impacted social dynamics. These resistances to policy showed just how fickle the bodies within the government are and have been in ensuring that equality or equity is made available with their lack of action towards social resistance to equitable policy shift. These dynamics have been informed by juxtaposed policies of the past that people wish to cling to because it sustains their power. Once the notion of power or access that would require that it be shared was presented, there was explicit unwillingness to follow law. This very notion of law was implemented so that privileged groups demanded allegiance to that maintained disenfranchisement. There proceeded to be practices of exclusion for African Americans with other institutions beyond education. These other forms of collusion were in redlining. Redlining being a practice that sectored black people in particular concentrated areas. This impacted the influence of their vote (also challenged and allowed through policy that took a significant amount of time to be enforced without overwhelming resistance socially and by those within law implementing bodies). It also impacted school districts that African Americans could live and receive home loans to purchase homes within[219]. Institutions worked in tandem to influence the manners by which policies could be circumvented and maintain status quo. Soon it became clear that housing value was correlated to the social capital of the marginalized or privileged bodies that lived in an area, understanding also that racial marginalized populations were attacked again by the pay gaps between them and those that held racial privilege. Property taxes soon became the mechanism by which resources were extended to particular school districts[220]. All these forces worked together to guarantee that resources not be spread equitably per student but was dictated by the minimal property value of racially marginalized populations. These marginalized populations received less pay through discrimination and had their homes valued to be less than from redlining. Redlining directly and disproportionately harmed communities of color which. These

---

[219] Nier III, Charles L. "Perpetuation of Segregation: Toward a New Historical and Legal Interpretation of Redlining Under the Fair Housing Act." J. Marshall L. Rev. 32 (1998): 617.

[220] Lipsitz, George. "The possessive investment in whiteness: Racialized social democracy and the" white" problem in American studies." American Quarterly 47, no. 3 (1995): 369-387.

practices, without doubt, influenced the trajectory of students' possibilities. African Americans and Native Americans were not the only groups impacted racially within the United States. Due to the Chinese Exclusion Act set in place, this again exploited the labor of Chinese and Chinese Americans, but also influenced the social valuation of the population's bodies[221]. In this, these Chinese exclusionary practices extended again into pay gaps, social perception, as well as within the institution of education. Chinese students were often emphatically denied access to the school system. *Tape vs. Hurley*[222] (1884) ruled that it was unconstitutional to discriminate against Chinese populations based on their racial identity. However, much like the desegregation policies created from *Brown vs. Board of Education*[223], there was significant resistance and outright refusal to accept Chinese students in California after the ruling was made. This exhibited again the miniscule de facto implementation of the policies and the explicit social acceptance for white bodies to refuse to follow the laws. These were statutes that racially marginalized populations were forced to accept that continued to marginalize them. Mexican Americans experienced similar practices of exclusion that also had to be challenged. In *Roberto Alvarez vs. Lemon Grove School Board*[224], the courts ruled that again it was unconstitutional to bar educational access to Mexican Americans simply for their identities.

Language continues to be used as a tool of power. Society by and large has been forced to be monolingual and demand that one language, English. English is the only cultural currency accepted for forms of communication. This practice excludes those who speak different languages primarily, those who have speech pathologies. Those that are differently abled in forms of communication such as the deaf or hard of hearing community. In this, we again subjugate particular populations to the margins while reifying the under-

[221] Daniels, Roger. Asian America: Chinese and Japanese in the United States since 1850. University of Washington Press, 2011.

[222] Noltemeyer, Amity L., J. U. L. I. E. Mujic, and Caven S. Mcloughlin. "The history of inequity in education." *Disproportionality in education: A guide to creating more equitable learning environments* (2012):4.

[223] Bell Jr, Derrick A. "Brown v. Board of Education and the interest-convergence dilemma." Harvard Law Review (1980): 518-533.

[224] Montoya, Margaret E. "A brief history of Chicana/o school segregation: One rationale for affirmative action." Berkeley La Raza LJ 12 (2000): 159.

standing of what "normal" means and who gets to be "normal". The nuanced thing about language differences is that yes, institutions sought to destroy the epistemologies of native tongues. English was also used as the dominant language to bar access to institutions that are set in place for social mobility. If services are not extended to ensure that those who speak different languages have access to monolingual institutions, then we in actuality continue to marginalize and filter out who can prosper in this country in a traditional sense. The problem here isn't necessarily the services and offered curriculum of English learning. It is the fact that we are expected to only speak English. We push forth a narrative that doesn't value expanding on the different forms of communication. The institution that is supposed to transmit knowledge, doesn't seem to care to give value to anything beyond the structured process of learning that benefits those that share lineage with colonial settlers. It's not a coincidence; these things are done with intention. We extend the "same" tools to everyone, understanding that equity and equality are not the same thing. However, knowing that the narrative of equality is such a strong one, institutions know that they don't have to do anything. The practice and theory of education and the lack of inclusive curriculum prevailed. We co-opt the term equality as if it isn't a form of violence. We behave as if the term hasn't been used to make social participants ignore historical destruction. Self-congratulatory congratulatory pats on the back were given for the tools they need to prosper. This access is given without admitting that their tools were taken away. These positive spins placed on limited progression hides behind the malevolent rhetoric that we all have the same things to prevail. We know fiscally, resource, and social capital wise that that simply is not true. Eventually policies were set in place due to the ruling of *Lau vs. Nichols*[225] (1974) where it was deemed that it was the school's responsibility to ensure that students had the language services that would give them the resources and tools to actively participate in matriculating through levels of education without being left behind. Not only this, we continue to marginalize based on gender in ways that reinforce patriarchal notions of education. Women were granted the right to

---

[225] Sugarman, Stephen D., and Ellen G. Widess. "Equal protection for non-English-speaking school children: Lau v. Nichols." California Law Review 62, no. 1 (1974): 157-182.

vote in 1920[226], but slaves were also free in 1863[227]. Everyone was supposed to have the right to vote after 1965[228]. These policies we have did take a long time to achieve, but just because a policy is in place does not mean we are done socially and that we don't have to pay close attention to practices of circumvention. In a gender role abiding, heterosexist, and patriarchal society, the treatment of Transgender and non-binary community continues to reify the value of masculinity and femininity. We continue to reinforce gender role expectations that come within those binaries[229]. It also reifies that one cannot reside outside of those binaries without harm to their trajectory in society but also in the context of educational school walls as well. Education for the most part has always been intended for cisgender white/ European males to gain the competencies they need to thrive. This is said with the understanding that income did impact access but not as much so for those who held other marginalized identities attacked by society as well as policy. Women have often been socially instructed to learn tools and skills that would make them good mothers and wives[230]. This process markedly assumes that all women are compulsorily heterosexual and that they in addition want to procreate. This alone influences the social expectancy of women and directly limits the scope of what they can do within a social, professional, or educational context. For as much as the woman is devalued- it is also realized that society depends on them to reify and obey social mores and socialize their children to do the same. Women were finally allowed access to educational institutions. Women were often only allowed or expected to finish school to a defined level that would prepare them to be a part of and raise a family that proliferated the "American way of life"- they were tasked with continuing the ostensible narrative. Women were not asked to critically think but to absorb and practice. As women gained access to higher education institu-

---

[226] Baker, Paula. "The domestication of politics: Women and American political society, 1780-1920." The American Historical Review 89, no. 3 (1984): 620-647.

[227] Hummel, Jeffrey. Emancipating slaves, enslaving free men: a history of the American civil war. Open court, 2013.

[228] Davidson, Chandler. Quiet revolution in the South: The impact of the Voting Rights Act, 1965-1990. Princeton University Press, 1994.

[229] Eccles, Jacquelynne S. "Gender roles and women's achievement-related decisions." Psychology of women Quarterly 11, no. 2 (1987): 135-172.

[230] Epstein, Barbara Leslie. "The Politics of Domesticity Women, Evangelism, and Temperance in Nineteenth-Century America." (1981).

tions[231], primary and secondary schools began to shift and understand that more women would be attending schools for longer. In this, the social concerns that women would go to school and try to obtain careers was thought to be an ill that could shake the moral fiber and gender norm dynamics of the country. Would education influence women to not obey their husbands? Who would raise the children? A pandemonium was set in place that's hard to fathom, but set in it did[232]. There were adamant challenges to women going to college and getting a career. In true American colonialist fashion, other institutions that held influence in the workforce ensured that women were paid less and made victims of employee discrimination as well as sexual harassment. This was done, to reify the notion that women essentially belonged at home and to strengthen the patriarchal narrative of a woman's usefulness. That usefulness often considered to solely be domestic. This extends more so with nonbinary and transgender people within workplaces. There are de jure policies in workplaces to protect against sex discrimination through Title VII in the Civil Rights Act of 1964[233]. The educational protection from discrimination of the basis of sex was meant to be protected with Title IX (1970)[234]. However, neither of these policies protects gender identity or sexual orientation from discrimination on a federal level and transgender, LGBTQQIA2S+, or non-binary persons continue to be marginalized on a national level. In this, we see the precariousness of marginalized identities persist without interruption to something we know impacts the trajectory of a person's ability to succeed, survive, or thrive. The ability to thrive is sought for, no matter what the level of one's educational attainment is. Non-bullying initiatives have taken place in some school districts and university campuses. However, any educational bodies still hold a common problem wherein there is a culture of doubt, rationalization, and failure to meet infraction with consequences. The culture of not believing or acting in defense and support of women,

[231] Solomon, Barbara Miller. In the company of educated women: A history of women and higher education in America. Yale University Press, 1985.

[232] Cockburn, Cynthia. In the way of women: Men's resistance to sex equality in organizations. No. 18. Cornell University Press, 1991.

[233] Blumrosen, Ruth G. "Wage Discrimination, Job Segregation, and the Title VII of the Civil Rights Act of 1964." U. Mich. JL Reform 12 (1978): 397.

[234] Klein, Susan S. Handbook for achieving sex equity through education. The Johns Hopkins University Press, 701 West 40th Street, Suite 275, Baltimore, MD 21211, 1985.

transgender folks, or people of marginalized sexual orientations when they express that they are being discriminated against in the classroom or on campus is not perfect by any means. There is also focus on peers and not as much attention is given to the discrimination practiced by educators or the school administration. We also find ways of minimizing the impact of discrimination by using words such as bullying rather than sexism, racism, homophobia, transphobia, or heterosexism. Why are we not calling these practices what they are? There is a real opportunity for the education system to systemically allow for name preference and pronouns to be integrated into electronic patch systems that connect to birth names[235]. However, most schools will not take that step to systemically shift oppression into even this degree of liberation. Most prolifically there are areas of conversation in reference to bathroom policies for transgender and non-binary persons in schools. In schools, many school boards refuse to identify gender non-conforming, non-binary, or transgender bodies as a protected class[236]. It is true that not allowing someone to be in a space that makes them feel comfortable is egregious, but we must go beyond the scope of a bathroom. If the social context is informing and validating invasive conversations against the inclusion of the non-binary, gender conforming, and the transgender community- how is this showing up in a larger scale?, How is this showing up in the work place that is the school? Each of these systemic and institutional scales influences the other and adds to the dominant narrative of discrimination. Schools could be a place to nullify discriminatory rhetoric, but in many regions it chooses not to. In many regions people, educators included, can be fired for simply identifying as queer[237]. So yes, the LGBTQQIA2S+ community can get married, but there is far more at stake than being a part of a matrimony intended to perpetuate interdependence on a partner rather than the state. Children are being discriminated against, bullied, being subjected to violence, holding fickle job security, and being kicked

---

[235] Beemyn, Brett Genny, Andrea Domingue, Jessica Pettitt, and Todd Smith. "Suggested steps to make campuses more trans-inclusive." Journal of gay & lesbian issues in education 3, no. 1 (2005): 89-94.

[236] Zemsky, Beth, and Ronni L. Sanlo. "Do policies matter?." New Directions for Student Services 2005, no. 111 (2005): 7-15.

[237] Lugg, Catherine A. "Sissies, faggots, lezzies, and dykes: Gender, sexual orientation, and a new politics of education?." Educational Administration Quarterly 39, no. 1 (2003): 95-134.

out of their homes. These problems begin in social and institutional spaces. The minimal educational system acknowledgement continues because they don't agree with what someone has privately decided or consensually decided to do with their bodies. To not have representation in educational policy explicit is another form of violent microinvalidation. We continuously perpetuate a monolithic idea of components that go into a body deemed acceptable. An immediate perception of monoliths ignores the harmful impacts of that ideology that is continuously overlooked. People are overlooked in ways that demand that people either hide who they are or assimilate in ways that feeds into the vitality of how American culture is supposed to be seen, understood, and digested no matter who it harms. We're teaching and reifying hate and violence rather than inclusion and safety. The educational institution is just as much to blame for that as any other institution we have in place if it doesn't proactively or reactively seek to interrupt that cyclical practice of exclusion and dispossession that it's known for so long. In addition, in the realm of gender, it became evidently clear that the impact of expected characteristics of masculinity proved itself to be harmful. These expectations were harmful in the ways in which males were expected to also fall in the parameters of traditional gender roles. These roles dictated who was expected to be a provider and what provision values meant more or less. A body devoid of demonstrative emotive expression beyond the scopes of traits attributed to masculinity such as anger is not healthy. There is also the expectation for males to not exhibit forms of vulnerability. Within educational systems where it's clear that no one knows *everything* the ability to ask for help being seen as "weak" is a problem. This relationship that society sees with associating asking for assistance with weakness has extensively impacted academic performance, behaviors, emotional underdevelopment, and negative emotional regulation[238].

On the identity of varying ability, the educational institution rarely allowed access to those with differing abilities-whether it is cognitive, physical, or emotional. Socially, the practice of hiding those of varying disabilities from society at large was an accepted dynam-

---

[238] Ghaill, Mac An. The making of men: Masculinities, sexualities and schooling. McGraw-Hill Education (UK), 1994.

ic[239]. Many people were never allowed to begin their journey of social mobility through the traditional educational model track because they were deemed to be contagious or distracting. Not only did this perpetuate the disposability of marginalized bodies, it also perpetuated the narrative that those with varying abilities had nothing to contribute to society. This narrative made many believe that those with varying abilities could not develop well enough to be considered a participant in a seemingly free choice and democratic society. In 1910, some measures were set in place to develop special education classes to assist those with disabilities with educational resources and accommodation so that they could attend school[240]. Individual Education Plans, (IEP's) were also mandated for those with varying abilities wherein a specialized learning plan was to be developed for those with varying abilities. These practices stemmed from the inclusions within the Children Act of 1975[241]. The Elementary and Secondary Education Act (ESEA) in 1965 was also put in place to provide federal funding for schools to implement programs for those of varying abilities[242]. *PARC vs Commonwealth of Pennsylvania* (1972) also ruled that school systems have to create programs for those with cognitive disabilities as well[243]. Lastly, the American Disabilities Act (ADA)of 1990, made it illegal refuse to create accessible modifications to public spaces for those with varying abilities[244]. These policies definitely demonstrate strides. We have to remember that these programs being set in place were also used for segregating. These programs limited the visibility of racially marginalized populations due to behavior or academic performance

[239] Ingstad, Benedicte. "The disabled person in the community: social and cultural aspects." International journal of rehabilitation research 13, no. 3 (1990): 187.

[240] Tomlinson, Sally. A sociology of special education (RLE Edu M). Routledge, 2012.

[241] Weintraub, Frederick J., Alan Abeson, and Jeffrey Zettel. "The End of Quiet Revolution: The Education for All Handicapped Children Act of 1975." Exceptional Children 44, no. 2 (1977): 114-128.

[242] Turnbull, Ann P. Exceptional lives: Special education in today's schools. Merrill/Prentice Hall, Order Department, 200 Old Tappan Rd., Old Tappan, NJ 07675., 1995.

[243] Daniels, Vera I. "Minority Students in Gifted and Special Education Programs The Case for Educational Equity." The Journal of Special Education 32, no. 1 (1998): 41-43.

[244] Yell, Mitchell L. The law and special education. Merrill/Prentice-Hall, Inc., 200 Old Tappan Road, Old Tappan, NJ 07675, 1998.

without seeking out and addressing the root of the issues that arose[245]. Progressive policies have come to fruition. However, the resources and the training available for educators and administrators to differentiate between the needs of students in ways that assist them in efficiently running a classroom by inclusive design has continuously failed to come to the fore. If policies exist, resources, competencies and oversight must follow. Spoon Theory[246] explains the fatigue felt from the community that holds varying abilities. We cannot task the youth and their guardians to continuously fight to shift the narrative alone. Those who work with and for students' ability to thrive are also tasked with ensuring that they gain the competencies necessary to advocate with those they hope to support. Often, the educators and the administrators don't have the resources or the capacity to give the students what they need even when they actually do want to try to do so in the public education school system. This is apparent especially if and when other marginalized identities are compounded from the communities' demographics' and exude the same despair of access to resources. Yes, if you have the fiscal resources to do so, these previously mentioned policies are great. However, if you do not have these resources and hold other marginalized identities, it becomes even harder to find a path that leads to one's heightened sense of self. It also makes it difficult to find inclusion in the narrative and the ability to gain the tools necessary to grow without hindrance.

The Byproducts of Institutionalized Oppression in the Educational System

If schooling is the entry way to molding the citizen as Labarre [247] stated, then the socio-political state of affairs lays on the blamed shoulders of the educational system. A system developed from the foundation of settler colonial practices of theft, control, exclusion

---

[245] Gay, Geneva. "Culturally responsive teaching in special education for ethnically diverse students: Setting the stage." International Journal of Qualitative Studies in Education 15, no. 6 (2002): 613-629.

[246] Miserandino, Christine. "The spoon theory." Retrieved December 25 (2010): 2013.

[247] Labaree, David F. "Public goods, private goods: The American struggle over educational goals." *American Educational Research Journal* 34, no. 1 (1997): 39-81.

and the educational reform response to the industrial revolution[248]. The form of schooling that was "revolutionized" came well equipped with biases. Biases that ensured that the social state of the marginalized had to inhabit a negative space devoid of upward mobility and were subjected to directive based positionality. In an environment that touts its support for linear progress, it proved difficult for marginalized populations to gain access to that linear track or to operate outside of those parameters freely. The ability to operate freely, in a way that didn't jeopardize access to needs that must be met to biologically survive proves difficult. The schooling system and mechanisms thereto were and are based on the mass consumed *a priori* that, as Tyack states, "Homogenizing American beliefs"[249] were paramount, expected, and should be sustained amidst increasing pluralism occurring in the United States. There-fore, the process of formalized schooling during the progressive era ensured that treatment of those who did not possess whiteness and those who did not align to "normal" standards of learning be deemed less efficient for societal prosperity. These educational reform policies not only hindered social mobility but also rein-forced the ideology of scientific racism through the practice of eugenics, developed by Galton[250]. Galton's ideas had a far reach to not only education, but also in the realms of public health, social interaction, systemic practices, and national policies.

In reference to the progressive era of education reform- the edu-cational institution was tasked with adjusting and orienting people to defined standards of learning. The system was also tasked with defining bodily categorization and ensuring that students could meet the needs of the labor force needs of the industrial revolu-tion[251]. The institution of education was removing itself from the optional participation of the privileged. Education in its infancy was

---

[248] Stoskopf, Alan. "Echoes of a forgotten past: Eugenics, testing, and educa-tion reform." In *The Educational Forum*, vol. 66, no. 2, pp. 126-133. Taylor & Francis Group, 2002.

[249] Tyack, David B. *The one best system: A history of American urban educa-tion.* Vol. 95, pp.180. Harvard University Press, 1974.

[250] Stoskopf, Alan. "Echoes of a forgotten past: Eugenics, testing, and educa-tion reform." In *The Educational Forum*, vol. 66, no. 2, pp. 126-133. Taylor & Francis Group, 2002.

[251] Becker, Gary S. "Human capital revisited." In Human Capital: A Theoreti-cal and Empirical Analysis with Special Reference to Education (3rd Edition), pp. 15-28. The University of Chicago Press, 1994.

focusing on philosophical and critical inquiry. The institution of education transformed into a space of capitalistic utility. Education's presence was used to develop human capital for industrial and capitalistic training and specialization of the individual within the masses. The industrial revolution catapulted our society into an arena never ventured into before. From this, differential learning was implemented as protocol where different populations were given access to particular categories and levels of learning. These categories and levels were based on what a person was expected to be capable of due to the identities they held. Those who were deemed less than socially, were not given access to higher levels of learning. These marginalized students were either dispossessed or extended education that significantly limited their trajectory. One can say that these limitations come from a colonialist and capitalist powerhouse that resides under the veil of patriotic altruism. One could also state that the purposes of differential learning were necessary to meet the needs of the growing economy and workforce (that inherently perpetuated –isms). However, we take self-agency away from developing youth to choose one's own path. We distort the actual purpose or critical inquiry and learning by articulating that it is more important for a person to be useful than to think. Society would rather define options for citizens rather than allow for one to make their own curricular decisions. It must be. It must be highlighted again, that education and schooling are distinct ideas, with distinct processes, goals and operate on different ideological planes that cannot be conflated. Education satiates exploration of thought; it explores the question "why?" with everything we encounter and keeps curiosity alive. Education never takes what is accepted as something that is always *right*. School is the body to which education has formally been placed into a system that extends the curriculum of "what" pupils need to learn to contribute to society in what is defined to be a "productive" way.

Those that aligned to the assigned learning practice of Goddard or Terman. Who were the originators of intelligence testing for social placement. Sadly, they were not concerned with learning simply for the sake of learning or learning to provide a pathway for children to obtain social mobility[252]. Schooling processes and the mechanisms of it that we know today, destroyed the unlimited possi-

---

[252] Snyderman, Mark, and R. J. Herrnstein. "Intelligence tests and the Immigration Act of 1924." American Psychologist 38, no. 9 (1983): 986.

bility of the institution becoming a place of equity, deconstruction of the status quo, and inclusion. Instead, the institution of education saw machines as opposed to human beings, and what these machines could do to benefit economic growth was its concern. The more educational administrators saw students as products, the easier it was to ignore their possibility dreams. In ignoring students, this veered the institution away from providing students with tools to achieve dreams they would aspire to and created no space for them to think about such dreams becoming reality.

If bodies were deemed "feebleminded", prone to "crime, poverty, and moral impropriety"[253], all these issues articulated could be directly attributed to the lack of educational access in a capitalistic society. Students were disposed of or it was administratively decided how far they could go in society. As a result, those who fell in the aforementioned categories, were only extended education that would allow them to be adequate at assigned levels of work. When we fail to acknowledge our atrocities, we allow capitalism to fold into *who* is taught and *who* is teaching. When we allow economic systems to dictate educational systems and *what* is taught and *how* curriculum is taught we devolve at an accelerated rate and repeat our ills of disenfranchisement repetitiously. The educational by-products of the industrial revolution exhibited to society the degree to which capitalism mattered. The learned advantage of institutional influence over education understood by companies and investors continues to insert itself into the dynamics of education. This insertion persistently today to produce products of the "what" they hope for students to master in practice, theory, as well as indoctrinated ideology[254]. Schools have been met with more demands for divestment from capitalistic sway within a public good such as education with a social justice oriented, intersectional, and equity and inclusion lens. There has been a surge of wealthy privileged bodies seeking to create a "talent pipeline"[255] . This pipeline indoctrinates

[253] Stoskopf, Alan. "Echoes of a forgotten past: Eugenics, testing, and education reform." In *The Educational Forum*, vol. 66, no. 2, p. 127. Taylor & Francis Group, 2002.

[254] Stolzenberg, Nomi Maya. "" He Drew a Circle That Shut Me out": Assimilation, Indoctrination, and the Paradox of a Liberal Education." Harvard Law Review (1993): 581-667.

[255] Olssen*, Mark, and Michael A. Peters. "Neoliberalism, higher education and the knowledge economy: From the free market to knowledge capitalism." Journal of education policy 20, no. 3 (2005): 313-345.

youth in ways that influences them to pledge their allegiance to perpetuating ideological disparity and oppression; to maintain capitalism and colonialism. The development of these pipelines is to seek to intergenerationally use developing youth as pawns to combat the movements pushing for the dissolution of wealth influence, capitalistic, and heteropatriarchal white supremacy in educational spaces. The hope of the capitalism and colonial oriented wealthy are to develop this talent with hopes that they concede to the enticement of neoliberalism. The tradeoff of is fiscal support to achieve certain measures of education and access to opportunities that aid in students' individual prosperity that will inevitably contribute to the added destruction of an already dilapidated structure. The institution of education remains not necessarily a perfected public good, but a place of social control and capitalist endeavors.

It's difficult to redirect ourselves back to the "why" of learning, knowledge, and education when we focus so much on what we are arbitrarily supposed to be learning. We focus on what we are told we are supposed to learn in order to achieve our maximum potential, all within a system that relentless marginalizes bodies.

Goddard and Terman discussed those who were considered to be "less than" to the point that they debated on whether "breeding" should be allowed. This suggestion of demographic extinction could be argued for on the premise of eugenics' false assertions alone[256]. Individuals of ethnicities differing from whiteness, genders differing from maleness, those who were not able bodied were all possible victims of marginalization. Those who do not comprehend in the same way as others were predestined for manual labor or an expectation of forced extinction or being made obsolete within society completely. This notion makes clear that the mental acuity of a person would be overlooked due to a label of their socially informed predestination. However, at no point did Goddard and Terman investigate the impropriety of those from Western European descent that were male and able bodied. Regulations don't always apply to the privileged. In this case, mental acuity and morality- "normalcy" are automatically assumed to be traits of Western European lineage.

---

[256] Stoskopf, Alan. "Echoes of a forgotten past: Eugenics, testing, and education reform." In *The Educational Forum*, vol. 66, no. 2, p. 129. Taylor & Francis Group, 2002.

The notion that particular racial and European ethnic groups were considered to be less mentally capable was more than appalling. The social climate of that era gave way to the motives of placing people on particular tracks of trajectory. Emphatically biased tests were developed and given validation soon after to complement the rank and file of marginalized populations. Terman and Thorndike push that "tests have told the truth" [257]. More accurately, tests have told the truth that those in power want to convey. You cannot score well on something that is constructed to benefit a particular group that has had access where others do not. The educational reformation system set up by Goddard and substantiated by Terman created assessments of intelligence quotients, disapproved of by the creator Binet, to be translated into educational systems [258]. These tests were designed for those they deemed to be less than (through race, gender, or economic class) to fail, again institutionalizing the practice of –isms and marginalization.

The means of developing assessments were drenched with undignified motives, careless research, and unsavory assigned terminology with no merit. One cannot possibly fathom a rational explanation beyond nefarious disenfranchisement in regards to the intentions of these normative ingrained practices within the educational system. Educational disenfranchisement for particular persons had been institutionalized, the gateways of education needed for prosperity had been locked. By systemically shutting out others within society from access to prosperity, whether it be a society in general or through particular mechanisms such as biased standardized tests. These historical heinous tactics resulted in the diminished amount of competition for those possessing identities of social capital or economic capital. Decreased competition through systemic barriers would ensure the privilege's entry and chance at a decent education as well as a higher trajectory in life. All the while, the comparative trajectories obscured, irrationally rationalized, unquestioned or ignored other marginalized populations.

When referencing eugenics, studies were conducted at Ellis Island focused on categorizing immigrants' competence by the Public

---

[257] Stoskopf, Alan. "Echoes of a forgotten past: Eugenics, testing, and education reform." In *The Educational Forum*, vol. 66, no. 2, p. 130. Taylor & Francis Group, 2002.

[258] Stoskopf, Alan. "Echoes of a forgotten past: Eugenics, testing, and education reform." In *The Educational Forum*, vol. 66, no. 2, pp. 126-133. Taylor & Francis Group, 2002.

Health Services[259]. From these studies, it becomes clear how educational reform approaches through multidimensional biased testing (class, race, gender and access) began and continued. These tests were working through subterfuge for unilateral validation with other government entities to ensure that significant obstacles were placed for those immigrating from non-Western European countries upon arrival. Governmental entities could bar their entry or limit their social mobility based on how they were ranked. This dimension of government took care of privileged persons incoming and within institutions. Education took, filtered, and ranked bodies and their trajectory of those who were already residing in the United States. We see how educational reform and its byproduct of testing measures gave birth to policy. Reform in practice oriented focus on containing and controlling those deemed to be "other". Those that were othered were thought to be incapable of contributing to or a threat to the homogeneity that the United States was attempting to create and fortify with influenced federal regulations such as the Immigration Restriction Act of 1924[260].

The policies and practices of the nation have been informed by slavery and xenophobia. The aspects of capitalism, complicit government entities, and educational reform became accomplices to the overall goal of controlling who has access to what through institutional practices. If the purpose of schooling, is to develop the model citizen, the implications of eugenics, shares the blame for the state that not only education is in today, but society in the United States context is in as well. The chance to make schools an entry way to the opportunity to build a competent workforce, appreciate pluralism, create an integrative curriculum that assessed achievement properly were possible goals that were squandered. Schools had the opportunity to design tracks that were of choice and equitable were. Instead, the opportunity was thrown away and the[261] education system at the turn of the century truly became the nexus of perpetuating an assessment based oppressive system. A system

---

[259] Stoskopf, Alan. "Echoes of a forgotten past: Eugenics, testing, and education reform." In *The Educational Forum*, vol. 66, no. 2, pp. 126-133. Taylor & Francis Group, 2002.

[260] Snyderman, Mark, and R. J. Herrnstein. "Intelligence tests and the Immigration Act of 1924." American Psychologist 38, no. 9 (1983): 986.

[261] Stoskopf, Alan. "Echoes of a forgotten past: Eugenics, testing, and education reform." In *The Educational Forum*, vol. 66, no. 2, pp. 126-133. Taylor & Francis Group, 2002.

that would perpetuate social injustice at the institutional level by leveraging the power of the privileged against the oppressed for centuries with capitalism and colonialism as its fuel. The fundamental essence of education's' purpose was dissolved. This is not to say that there aren't anecdotal instances of school success. However, these instances are more so made possible by the overtime of educators and administrators through dedication, to see students succeed rather than the increase of governmental support for these initiatives monetarily or with policies.

The progressive era is where we as a nation had space for reform and failed miserably. We failed by trying to sustain status quo power dynamics, maintain supremacist beliefs, and increase manual labor efficiency. In doing so, socialized ourselves to be citizens that cater to fueling the longevity of the aforementioned. Once again through reformation, we created the same product. That product being the construction of an empire on the backs of human beings needed to automate the systems of oppression by doing one thing. That one thing being, not providing equitable access to education through the means of scientifically invalid pseudo-scientific rationalizations.

The Guise of Concern and the Practice Measurement

The theme of governmentality and neoliberalism [262] arise often when we discuss the institution of education. These concepts were used as a guide to understanding how these two ideologies have led to the perpetuated failure. This failure has also led to gross negligence, inequity, questionable motives and hybridity (public and private mechanics) of our educational system under the guise of accountability and measure[263]. All systems, however, need public buy in (albeit from those with enough capital influence to participate in purchase).

Standardized testing and intelligence testing as bias as they are, do multiple things at once. The simultaneous actions geared to marginalize, substantiate its use under ostensible concern, and reify narratives. The system also reinforces status quo perceptions and expectations of particular bodies in these tests' administration, evaluation, and content. We hear the terms "failing schools" often, but with limited resources and bias testing that concerns itself with

---

[262] Taubman, Peter Maas. *Teaching by numbers: Deconstructing the discourse of standards and accountability in education.* Routledge, 2010.

[263] Garrison, Mark J. *A measure of failure: The political origins of standardized testing.* SUNY Press, 2009.

recitation over comprehension, it seems more accurate that the institution of education has failed the schools, the educators, *and* the students. Those who make decisions about the dynamics of education from a federal level downward have influence and information of the historical trend of less than ideal practice being extended to the community at large. One must realize that standardized testing is but another tool of oppression that works for the educational institution in tandem with other institutions to ensure control or self-destruction. By self-destruction I mean that these institutions were not designed to be inclusionary, they were designed to maintain a particular image and narrative. From this, looking specifically at education- we see that society has destroyed, invalidated, made unverifiable, and taken away hope. Society has also devalued cultural components and affects of marginalized populations so that they would not be included in the development of the institution of education's dynamics. However, as access began to increase, albeit for reasons beyond "equality", the system starts to buckle indicated that it was either never meant to handle or function at that level of capacity due to its rank and file procedures or it was designed to combust. It combusts because it's dynamics are working against the grain of its original intentions of exclusionary mechanics. We see public schools today and understand that the government isn't really looking for solutions, the solutions have to be an overhaul and that isn't the direction that reform is moving in. The passions of the department of education seem to be implicitly pushing and encouraging people to move closer to the acceptance of charter schools wherein federal dollars could be used. However, whether conservative liberal or somewhere in between, the founders could teach who they want how they want. Seeing the destructive environment that the public-school system has become it doesn't at first glance seem like a bad idea until you realize that some schools could indoctrinate students in a hateful way. But this indoctrination won't be regulated in exchange for educational access. Charter educational mechanisms take the culpability and responsibility of education being a public good completely away. Power must be taken away from institutions so that government can't walk away from what they put in place and consequences that cause cultural, social and academic destruction. In addition, if one doesn't have access to a charter school and had to rely on public education- what would become of those students? It is true that particular schools do not have to go through testing standards. However, who's to say that access, funding, transportation, and enrollment caps won't be used to marginalize the same bodies again. At present the only people that can avoid standardized testing are some charter and private schools. However, is it not peculiar that the only people that can avoid these biased forms of testing are the ones who have the privilege of attending school elsewhere? Is it not interesting that the privilege is not so much in access to education or schools as much as the privilege dwells in where you are and have access to be educated? Public education is seen as a disadvantage in cultural capital. Public education is also where standards are implemented to indoctrinate based on rubrics that hinder the social mobility of those with marginalized identities. Private and charter schools could circumvent these regulations of standards but public schools cannot. Public schools' resources are threatened by not the grades of the students, but the standardized test score results. Resources per student are based on the property value of the homes in their neighborhood over any other factor. The support extended to these schools remain miniscule at best due to social segregation and the perpetuation of "–isms".

Taubman and Garrison make clear that the readiness of the nation to latch on to standardization has been fueled by our preoccupation and reaction to provoked fear [264] and the ambiguous definition "of failure"[265]. We take the taught importance of competition from the classroom, to other social spaces, and eventually use that logic in a global and transnational context.

As Garrison[266] asserts "standardized tests originated in a crucible of failure"[267]. We have developed a culture of auditing rather than finding innovative ways to audit to ensure that we're achieving our goals[268]. Who stands to gain anything from our fear based "preoc-

---

[264] Taubman, Peter Maas. *Teaching by numbers: Deconstructing the discourse of standards and accountability in education*.p.129. Routledge, 2010.

[265] Garrison, Mark J. *A measure of failure: The political origins of standardized testing*. SUNY Press, 2009.

[266] Garrison, Mark J. *A measure of failure: The political origins of standardized testing*. SUNY Press, 2009.

[267] Garrison, Mark J. *A measure of failure: The political origins of standardized testing*. p.1. SUNY Press, 2009.

[268] Taubman, Peter Maas. *Teaching by numbers: Deconstructing the discourse of standards and accountability in education*.pp.96-106. Routledge, 2010.

cupation with failure"[269]. Failure, wherein, we look outward rather than inwards regarding our educational system. Not pledging allegiance to educational processes of standardizations would leave us in a state of vulnerable peril if we can't redefine educational value in nontraditional methodology. We delved deeper into understanding that the educational institution has become a marketplace. This is a marketplace that produces what's deemed useful for society to continue operating at a satisfactory level. The educational marketplace makes deals only with those deemed appropriate so that they can automate its functionality and processes.

The United States is built on an image and those that live at the lower rungs of its hierarchy[270] are less and less disillusioned by the clear motives of the educational institution to sustain power and allow it to remain in the hands of a few. When governmentality[271] took control of the education system it was because, yes it has its capitalistic focus, but it was also noticed that education had become and continue to be used as a form of political and social power[272]. The common school started this and standardization completed the process. The hardest thing about standardization is that its rhetoric "sounds good" but it places us in a similar fugue state as most of our equality based social policies and amendments. It creates a de jure environment and its implicit and de facto actuality and implications are insidious [273] and harder to explicitly pinpoint in its modes of disenfranchisement. This is a substantial dilemma when contemplating solutions. How can we argue with "equality" based policies?

Governmentality "organizes the conduct of conduct… at the macro and micro level…focused on its own self-regulation"[274] with the populace as a whole as testing field. Government consistently tests

---

[269] Garrison, Mark J. *A measure of failure: The political origins of standardized testing.* p.1. SUNY Press, 2009.

[270] Garrison, Mark J. *A measure of failure: The political origins of standardized testing.* p.20. SUNY Press, 2009.

[271] Taubman, Peter Maas. *Teaching by numbers: Deconstructing the discourse of standards and accountability in education.*pp.96. Routledge, 2010.

[272] Garrison, Mark J. *A measure of failure: The political origins of standardized testing.* p.8. SUNY Press, 2009.

[273] Garrison, Mark J. *A measure of failure: The political origins of standardized testing.* p.104. SUNY Press, 2009.

[274] Taubman, Peter Maas. *Teaching by numbers: Deconstructing the discourse of standards and accountability in education.* pp.97. Routledge, 2010.

the field of education and takes no regard of how this affects sociological groups unless it is the groups of the privileged. Standardization ensures the positive trajectory of historically favored groups.
Standardization does not ensure that students receive the same
quality of education, nor does it ensure that those that comprehend
differently or have not been exposed to certain issues or content
succeed. Standardization measures practiced without care or space
for adjustment and only adherence does the exact opposite of its
ostensible intention of ensuring success of pupils within ostensible
intention of ensuring the success of pupils within the systems of
education to which the practices are housed.

Governmentality sought to rule the masses, and other educational
reforms sought to produce functional citizens for the "greater good"
of the nation. However, the educational system within the United
States context ignored the individualized needs of the learner until
the concept of neoliberalism surfaced in a very unique way. Neoliberalism made an excuse for some students to succeed over others,
but at no point in time was equity a factor in configuring this concept. If one received no access to start a race, how could they possibly win or finish well? If one received a later start because they had
to wait for societal barriers to be lifted, even a small bit, how could
they possibly win?   Neoliberalism essentially means every person
for themselves and their own interests. If this is a sensibility that we
ingrain within our educational system- what's the point in playing
in a rigged game? Standardized testing solidified favor forever being
extended to particular social groups and blamed those who consistently failed to succeed based on school standard, by citing that
these populations were not adequately investing in their own fu-
tures. Conversely, in the interest of the educator- it is more favorable
to maintain a job and implement testing rather than resist or find
creative ways around these standards invested in, in the interest of
the government. If government wanted to maintain power and injustice within the overall social context, it was in its best interest to insti-
tutionalize standardized testing. The day the educational system
became a place of mere unfair competition, was the day it emphatically failed itself.

I don't blame the citizens for the state that the educational system
is in. Accountability measures being institutionalized was a successful tactic in maintaining power in specific pockets. Neoliberalism is not just a concept that affects educators and students, but it

is also a concept that I believe Horace Mann[275], an educational reformist, had in mind himself along with all of his predecessors and successors in advocacy for accountability techniques from these approaches of measuring accountability. Yet, the state gained more control over the educational system and created a factory of unjust culture, but it also gave those who "rehabilitated" the educational system the fuel to boost their own positionality and legacy[276]. The standardization of the educational system has also created a marketplace mentality for those who provide and create tests through contracts. This partnership between institutions and corporations are incentivized to maximize survivability of the government and economic systems set in place.

Through accountability measures, what we did was make sure that particular persons succeeded and that others would fail. I suppose Mann thought this was some sort of balance. Maybe he was unconcerned with consequences. Maybe the American people were so seized by the fear that their way of life in the dream projected would be disturbed, that all the pieces just fell into their places to lay what seems to be an unbreakable foundation of broken and broke-in practice.

The negligence of the government within the educational institution has put us to shame[277]. Our nation is at risk and has been ever since the system catered to economics and prejudice more than actual learning. If it were set in place to develop a citizen in a democratic society, it definitely did not ingrain the democratic process into its operation. Today we have administrators and public appointees in positions to where their authority cannot be touched. We have students perpetually pushed to the sidelines without addressing our abhorrent history of marginalization. We have educators who simply gave up because of the threat of losing their jobs, as they see their profession be destroyed by systemic processes. The measures put in place to "protect" us, is leading to our eventual demise of intellectual creativity. But maybe that was the intention; it most certainly was the impact. So, as we measure ourselves on

[275] Messerli, Jonathan. *Horace Mann: A Biography.* Knopf Books for Young Readers, 1972.
[276] Garrison, Mark J. *A measure of failure: The political origins of standardized testing.* p.98. SUNY Press, 2009
[277] Taubman, Peter Maas. *Teaching by numbers: Deconstructing the discourse of standards and accountability in education.* pp.137-139. Routledge, 2010.

predefined rubrics of learning, we can't see creation, critical thought, we can only see how well we paint by numbers[278]. We measure students and measure our educators, but at no point did the system measure itself and acknowledge just how far down the rabbit hole we have gone. We watch as intentions to revise institutional practices are continuously rolled out without public consultation. If we don't eradicate the testing rubrics or its foundational motives, I'm not sure we'll ever know what equitable access to success even looks like.

The Release of Cynicism and the Orientation Towards Possibility

The idea of transformation is used as a rhetorical tool within the educational system but still remains to be an idea that has rarely trickled down into practice unless discussed in the context of efficiency or mobility via competition[279]. There is no "love story" [280] for education because we don't get to create by common practice. There is no language of appreciation for possibility or growth beyond measurement by a standard. There's no transformation in any other form than what the educational institution sorts you to have the possibility to achieve as it holds the power of access. At present, we're faced with a lack of engagement, a lack of reciprocity, and a lack of vision. What this means for our educational schooling system, is that we continuously sought to make adjustments to a system. A system that is not now, nor was it ever meant to be able to create and cultivate an environment where the true essence of transformation and language concerning it is made possible. We never made space within the institution of education for those conversations and consequently have made no strides in institutionalizing the notion of transformation.

The way we speak about education limits the manners by which it can be changed. Rose states, "I worry that the dominant vocabulary about schooling limits our shared respect for the extraordinary nature of thinking and learning, and lessens our sense of social

---

[278] Taubman, Peter Maas. *Teaching by numbers: Deconstructing the discourse of standards and accountability in education.* Routledge, 2010.

[279] Martin, Jane Roland. *Educational metamorphoses: Philosophical reflections on identity and culture.*p.6.Rowman & Littlefield, 2007.

[280] Rose, Mike. *Why school?: Reclaiming education for all of us.* New Press, The, 2014.

obligation"[281]. Maybe that was the intended goal when we look at the nation's timeline inclusions that we are privy to. As Rose states, "public discourse, heard frequently enough and over time, affects the way we think, vote, and lead our lives" [282]. Maybe we used this power for control and never intended for it to be used for growth, freedom or liberation. The institutionalization of education from its inception robbed us of our ability to dream, imagine alternative possibilities, or hold ourselves accountable to seek them out while it directed the way we vote, follow laws, or how we are to be as a citizen,

The mere fact that the notion of transformation seems implausible, unconscionable, unfathomable is a heavy burden to hold in what we as a society can realize or actualize as attainable. However, we have to push back in a system that we speak about in such a "mundane and prosaic"[283] way in new ways that shifts the common place of accepting the educational system for what it is. We must replace the narrative and direct actions of discovering what education can evolve to be. We make changes to components of our educational system when we know that our one size *should* fit all approach has never been effective or equitable. Due to these metaphorical sizes not fitting, we're consistently or ostensibly trying to clean up the mess that our educational system always makes.

The other aspect of language when discussing education is that we lack the practice of acknowledging the achievements of growth in a substantive way. The absence of that positive reinforcement for just being in school because you *want* to be there is lost in a system of required automation with the threat of punitive consequence if not complied with. We also fail to uplift conversations consistently concerning why a student *doesn't* want to or *can't* be at school. From this negligence we minimize our chances of finding ways to deconstruct those barriers in a way that hears the voice of the students, the educators as well as administrators. We also minimize our opportunities to find ways to provide support to shift the perception of school with substantive and accessible changes. We see

---

[281] Rose, Mike. *Why school?: Reclaiming education for all of us.* p. 29. New Press, The, 2014.

[282] Rose, Mike. *Why school?: Reclaiming education for all of us.* p. 29. New Press, The, 2014.

[283] Martin, Jane Roland. *Educational metamorphoses: Philosophical reflections on identity and culture.* p.6. Rowman & Littlefield, 2007.

school as something "as inevitable as death and taxes"[284]. We don't talk about school in a way that praises education for education's sake. We talk about school in a way that only pushes forward what will happen to you if you don't "do" school in the various ways prescribed. It's hard to love something, that doesn't love you back or even notices or cares about the *way* or *what* you think. School is tasked to get you to intake information. This process of intake rarely leaves space for processing unless you have the opportunity to get into college, and even then, that critical thought is not necessarily an expectation. There's no doubt that everyone doesn't want to attend college. However, we fail to even wholeheartedly discuss the disproportionate validity given to education extended outside formal school walls, in an autodidactic sense. We fail to request that those who built competencies elsewhere show their competence through a vetting process that values nontraditional education processes. It's hard to love something that doesn't let you love yourself and your own gumption because it has to consistently be verified in or outside school walls in ways that most times aren't applicable to the goals that pupils seek to achieve. It's hard to love something that thrives on competition. It's hard to love something that thrives on you being "better" than your peers so that you won't get left behind. Left behind based on "number of years of schooling...how many grade levels completed...hours devoted to homework or the number of books read, math problems solved, spelling bee words memorized..."[285]. We focus so much on competition that we don't realize that that form of competition lives in the blood of our society. We train developing youth to practice that form competition from primary school onward, furthering its pervasive presence in our society generation by generation. There's no appreciation or love in that form of competition. However, there is the creation of a culture that defines normal ways and content of learning as well as normalization of unquestioned marginalization and disposability. If we limit the ways that we speak about education, we limit the possibilities of not only the educational system but also the self-efficacy of everyone impacted by it. We have to see beyond the scope of what we have. We have to discuss what we want, find ways to achieve those things, learn from our historical ills, and in-

---

[284] Martin, Jane Roland. *Educational metamorphoses: Philosophical reflections on identity and culture.* p.9. Rowman & Littlefield, 2007.

[285] Martin, Jane Roland. *Educational metamorphoses: Philosophical reflections on identity and culture.* p.6. Rowman & Littlefield, 2007.

clude all voices in the transformation of what we want education to be. These steps must be taken forward if we want or think education can or should be inclusively institutionalized. If this is attempted, we could redefine what the responsibilities of the government are in providing and protecting equitable resources for this public good.

Transformation has the ability to shock and change the composition of the educational institution and its structure and influence on society. Transformation has the ability to shift the dynamics of society as a whole as well. But the transformation has to be collectively catalyzed and sustained in a way that builds a new infrastructure for schools. An infrastructure that demands self-critique and change when a functionality or mechanism and is no longer working as opposed to ignoring problems just because the machine is still running. We cannot interchange the terms "running" and "working" if we understand working to be comprised of effectiveness and inclusion rather than solely the idea of running regardless of who and what is left out. As Martin states, "the great transformation education brings about in people have a cultural as well as a personal or psychological dimension"[286]. In that respect, why would we not transform the systemic dynamics of school where education has the ability to eradicate the ways in which the system can be harmful to those aforementioned dimensions of being? We lose sight of seeing the philosophical as having the possibility of tangibility. We are more invested in sustaining our educational practices of today unfortunately. This investment is so deep that those who are immersed in the educational system have become collateral damage. Students, teachers, and administrators have become collateral damage through trial and error because we haven't given ourselves the space to think bigger. We haven't "pay[ed] attentions to the experience of going to school"[287] and used that information to make substantive institutional changes. If we pay attention to voices of school experiences, these voices could flow upwards to educators and administrators, and school boards. However, this removes responsibility from the educational institution to provide resources or deconstruct some of the policies that stand in

---

[286] Martin, Jane Roland. *Educational metamorphoses: Philosophical reflections on identity and culture.* p.8. Rowman & Littlefield, 2007.

[287] Rose, Mike. *Why school?: Reclaiming education for all of us.* p. 32. New Press, The, 2014.

the way of educational transformation[288]. The institution of education hinders but claims no liability for the consequences of its mechanic practice, parameters, and/or regulations.

The educational system as we understand it today, doesn't allow administrators or educators the opportunity to create without threat, to see beyond a standardized score. Many of the policies placed on schools are ones that come with detrimental consequences if not adhered to. Despite the vociferousness of many, those voices most affected by educational policy are never truly given the power to create a system or environment that they love. The discussion on how to achieve that kind of environment is silenced. This silence continues because there are no mechanisms in place that even uplift the validity of the idea to give those most impacted a voice that's heard, absorbed, and acted upon.

The institution of education has given no incentive for those impacted by it, to love it. This is the era of educational disenchantment. The only incentive in the education system is that it's requirement and successful matriculation through it gives one access to mobility or allows one to maintain their job. Again, that's not reciprocity, that's extortion. I'm not suggesting that education should be optional for K-12. However, I am suggesting that the way that it is structured in schools is not ideal. Students, educators, administrators, and parents alike should be in a relationship with the educational system whereby they give the best they have in the ways that they are capable. Each party's commitment could help parents, students, teachers, and administrators define what growth is or looks like, how it can be measured or if it needs to be. We don't have that now and to say we do and blame those who slip through its strategically located systemic cracks for their own downfall is absolutely absurd. The system failed some of those within it before they even enrolled. Students are not encouraged to create, they are encouraged to practice "obedience and conformity"[289]. Administrators are not encouraged to create; they are encouraged to implement. Teachers are not encouraged to innovate, nurture, or cultivate; they are encouraged to carry out curriculum that ensures

---

[288] Theoharis, George. "Social justice educational leaders and resistance: Toward a theory of social justice leadership." Educational administration quarterly 43, no. 2 (2007): 221-258.

[289] Martin, Jane Roland. *Educational metamorphoses: Philosophical reflections on identity and culture.* p.22. Rowman & Littlefield, 2007.

success rates with tests. Parents are not encouraged to speak up or push back against policies they don't agree with, they're encouraged to make sure their children attend.

From the educational system's failure to make space for those within it to have the opportunity to create and to love their creation, it goes without saying that the educational environment does not cultivate, grow, or contribute to creating a love story. School has "devolve[d] to procedures, to measures and outputs that constrain what gets taught, how it's taught, and how we define what it means to be an educated person"[290]. Each love story, as it is in life, is unique to those within that relationship. However, the environment has to be ripe to even imagine love's possibility. I know that saying love story can come off as sounding trite or trivial. However, Love isn't based on a designed standard, for standards only "attempt to reduce education to its lowest common denominator"[291]. Love is based on negotiation, appreciation, acknowledgement of differ-ence, and the ability to work through challenges amidst complica-tions because of commitment. Love stories in education do exist. It's just unfortunate that they are seen so minimally that those sto-ries are categorized as phenomena and the search for that love story isn't institutionalized to be uniquely developed for each student that enters the halls of a school.

The question remains for the pragmatic mind as to how we can create something tangible that can be loved, that makes room for creation. A creation that speaks about education in a language that acknowledges growth outside of parameters. We simply do not have this conversation enough for it to gain traction and tangible comes, but that's not to say that it isn't possible. The way we have been indoctrinated is to believe that if something is not palatable due to its lack of existence in previously accepted archetypes, it is not de-serving of mental energy to create. Sometimes discussion and lan-guage shift is where we start. When we speak about things as if they could be possible, we shed ourselves of the limitations that we placed on our own minds. And when our minds are free, who knows what can be made tangible? In conclusion, I'm left with one last question and asking it from a place open to its possibility. The

---

[290] Rose, Mike. *Why school?: Reclaiming education for all of us.* p. 27. New Press, The, 2014.

[291] Martin, Jane Roland. *Educational metamorphoses: Philosophical reflec-tions on identity and culture.* p.6. Rowman & Littlefield, 2007.

question being, what would it take to create an educational system where our intention was to ensure that we convey that cultivating the development of a person was a priority *and* "not purely intellectual or cognitive"[292] based, but holistic?

Media

One thing about media that is being discussed but not nearly enough, is how media in its infinite forms has solidified its place in society as a staple institution. It is hypothesized that more exploration of this conversation has not been had because of its ebbs, flows, and continual transformations and various mediums. However, to operate within our society as if media is not an institution that has a colossal influence on our lives is irresponsible[293]. Media is how we gain access to what is going on in our greater society. Media also shows that it fails to represent the marginalized in ways that don't perpetuate and enhance stereotypes and stigmas set in place by the power dynamic of colonialism on a mainstream level.

After the Spanish American war and competition of journalistic consumerism as well as influence, it was clear what kind of sway that media has on perceptions of current events. A war was started because of journalistic competition and continued to spin out of control into sensationalism[294]. In a capitalistic society- truth and facts are rarely the most important proponents and journalistic integrity has always been dubious at best. When propaganda sells papers, the majority of society buys into the perpetuation of oppression based language. However, the consequence of this is that media has the power and the ability to mold minds, to plant seeds, and to continue to nurture oppression from news to societal behavior as can be evident post-9/11 as well[295]. As we continue to report factual news, it is seen that our society cares more for sensationalism than the humanity of a people and the full scope of a story with vetted facts in tow to inform one's position. However, we also intake

[292] Martin, Jane Roland. *Educational metamorphoses: Philosophical reflections on identity and culture.* p.12. Rowman & Littlefield, 2007.

[293] Kellner, Douglas, and Jeff Share. "Toward critical media literacy: Core concepts, debates, organizations, and policy." *Discourse: studies in the cultural politics of education* 26, no. 3 (2005): 369-386.

[294] Greer, Chris. "Crime and media: understanding the connections." *Criminology* 2 (2009): 177-203.

[295] Alsultany, Evelyn. *Arabs and Muslims in the Media: Race and Representation after 9/11.* nyu Press, 2012.

information form sources that agree with our moral and intellectual positioning and have the ability to discard anything that goes against the grain of those positions and beliefs. Facts, sensationalism, or neither- we believe what we want to believe no matter what information we are met with.[296].

Due to lack of access of marginalized populations within institutions, the treatment or barricades were no less for the institution of media. Mainstream media has been stabilized on the table of Eurocentrism and fails to broaden its scope[297]. Considering that white cisgender male ownership of media proliferated for centuries, this alone is not a surprise. However, let's broaden the conversation even more- our representations, perpetuation of stereotypes and dehumanization as well as appropriation has expanded to music, film, and social media[298].

As we continue to talk about music and molding perceptions on a Eurocentric basis we make it clear in the United States context that marginalized people that produce music are seen as vagrants, less than, or inappropriate in comparison to Eurocentric baselines of normalcy[299]. We are hypervigilant to music produced by marginalized groups and continue to demonize them and perpetuate stereotypes complicit with bodies such as the FCC in a country that claims censorship is unacceptable. It is also clear that when music is appropriated or co-opted or even accepted into mainstream, it is dependent on the gatekeepers such as radio stations. Gatekeepers decide what is in and what's out and ignores the theft or colonization of a genre if a hegemonic body is the face of it.

When we discuss movies and television, it is very clear that marginalized bodies were not allowed to be seen as anything other than a monolith or the embodiment of a socialized perceptual stereotype. Thespians of marginalized communities remain to be type cast into archetypes such as the humorous black person without

---

[296] Wilson II, Clint C., Felix Gutierrez, and Lena Chao. *Racism, sexism, and the media: The rise of class communication in multicultural America.* Sage, 2003.

[297] Kincheloe, Joe L., Shirley R. Steinberg, Nelson M. Rodriguez, and Ronald E. Chennault, eds. *White reign: Deploying whiteness in America.* Palgrave Macmillan, 2000.

[298] Cross, Ian. "Music, cognition, culture, and evolution." *Annals of the New York Academy of sciences* 930, no. 1 (2001): 28-42.

[299] Shohat, Ella, and Robert Stam. *Unthinking Eurocentrism: Multiculturalism and the media.* Routledge, 2014.

intellect, or the damsel in distress, or the suicidal queer body. There are minimal attempts by mainstream media to represent people as multidimensionally as white cisgender able bodied people. Often sexism continues to rear its head in forms whereas an "unattractive" male gets the "gorgeous woman". This sexist story line reifies the levels and archetypes, modes of attractiveness, who can navigate it and who cannot. Who isn't allowed to be an archetype of access could be seen as women who have a larger body size or don't fit into the Western European perception and ideology of beauty that has been placed on us all[300] . Think of how people internalize something they see or don't see every day. Think about how people compare themselves to media's rhetoric of normalcy. Think about how we reinforce narratives of "boys just being boys" or only men being in positions of power or not seeing racially marginalized bodies at all[301]. The impact of white bodies portraying people of color, of cisgender people portraying transgender or non-binary bodies, of able bodied persons portraying people of varying abilities also push a form of normalcy. Are there no marginalized thespians? We know there are, and we ignore that authentic representation and on ramp to that representation career wise as if the public wouldn't notice. But it's always been noticed- it's just not being accepted anymore.

This is not to say that some strides have not been made in news and information sharing or more mainstream representation but the residual impacts of colonial marginalization remain clear and still disproportionality decides what is acceptable or unacceptable. This is where social media comes in, and for as much as it created an outlet for other voices typically marginalized from mainstream to be heard, mainstream media and capitalism has tried to infiltrate it as well. There has been considerable resistance to hegemony and marginalized expression in online spaces developed for empowerment, but much like any coin there are two sides. The ability to operate under anonymity with commentary creates a safety net for those who are marginalized. However, this anonymity feeds the fertile soil of social media with the ability for hegemonic groups to

---

[300] Shohat, Ella, and Robert Stam. *Unthinking Eurocentrism: Multiculturalism and the media.* Routledge, 2014.

[301] Shohat, Ella, and Robert Stam. *Unthinking Eurocentrism: Multiculturalism and the media.* Routledge, 2014.

victimize themselves, harass and terrorize marginalized communities through hateful rhetoric[302].

Marginalized communities still continue to thrive on Facebook, Tumblr, and alternative news sources and even with podcasts[303]. However, for every outlet that could be a refuge or a space of building empowerment there are those who want society to remain the same. This keeps perceptions intact about marginalized bodies because of their unwillingness to share power. The internet has become a multidimensional minefield, but one that is entered at any rate because the news we gain from mainstream- just is not enough. Media codes words of oppression into forms of digestible acceptability and fails to reframe the narrative. It pushes words that invalidate people's experiences, places some expectation of normalcy on the table, and uses semantics that directly correlate to stereotyped perceptions of marginalized bodies. These perceptions become imprinted on the public. The news doesn't use the words "gang" or "thugs" on white bodies[304]. We use the words civil disobedience with intention of molding perception. Media will identify a body as transgender and use the wrong gender pronoun. Media will legitimize street harassment and domestic violence towards women, non-binary folks, especially people of color. Media will completely erase the varying abilities of people if they aren't white. Everyone can be humanized that meets a rubric of acceptability, but what about those that don't? Media has a lot of work to do but because their work is in most instances economically driven, they often see no need to make any changes. We can only wait to see what shifting to online platforms will prove for the future depending on our neuroplasticity, us believing what we want to believe, and us being in control of what we digest.

---

[302] Gagliardone, Iginio, Danit Gal, Thiago Alves, and Gabriela Martinez. Countering online hate speech. UNESCO Publishing, 2015.

[303] Blevins, Jeffrey Layne. "Counter-hegemonic media: Can cyberspace resist corporate colonization." *Cyberimperialism?: Global Relations in the New Electronic Frontier* (2001): 140-151.

[304] Steuter, Erin, and Deborah Wills. *At war with metaphor: media, propaganda, and racism in the war on terror.* Lexington Books, 2009.

Chapter 5

Here We Go Again:
Cyclical Oppression

There have been a lot of theories that have deductively or inductively come to the fore to guide social justice movements from feminist, queer, to critical race theory. However, those that lead to molds and models will typically or inevitably, have gaps because social justice is an arena of continual transformation and flux. There is credit that is due to those who chose to start *somewhere* in theory or practice to learn from faux pas of practice or in reassessment of theoretical development. However, that does not negate the cyclical oppression in the models pressed forward and adopted by following movements. Some practitioners may fill gaps in reevaluating their mode of implementation by reframing its ideological foundations and a theorist may need to fill gaps by assessing for unthought-of variables. Variables that don't make the theoretical framework of its triangulation operate as theorized in application. This means that building and deconstruction responsibly continues or should continue to occur. This means that we need to continue visioning what a future could look like as our ultimate goals as opposed to being confined to previous perceptions of a reality that we have the ability to alter. On either side, theorist or practitioner, both have fallen short historically in its visioning phase of what could be unless we focus on the worst-case scenarios that bring us together. At some point, defense just isn't going to work anymore, if it already has in any way. Much like basketball, if we know the "opponents" we face continuously use the same practices and fake to the left and ultimately go right, we need to be prepared defensively as a team that always "wins", but what are we going to do when we get the ball? Maybe we have to walk away from the game.

We often fall victim, in social justice movements of action or in thought, to the colonial preconception of what is obtainable and those constrictions lead to the limitation of our movements' trajectory as well as our own entrapment. It is not solely the practice of moments in social justice. Moreover, the ability and viability of envisioning a dignified future for the marginalized among the privileged should eventually lead to the indelible conversation of allyship. That solidarity that in application- has caused rifts in our social justice movements due to fragility and a lack of articulation of realities that the marginalized experience. We can form a framework for social justice all we want. Until we deal with the issues of theory, practice, and solidarity, our visions retain no operating system because we have to create it ourselves. Thus far, we have been mentally and physically operating in the system of colonization that is not fruitful, or productive for our movements in the future, lest we all fall back into the cycle of oppression that we live in now. In this, we move closer to an operating system that is automated by the marginalized. We disenfranchise each other based on the same colonial heteropatriarchal white supremacist frameworks we have lived under for centuries in scaffolded body capitol order.

Emerging Theory

More often than not, we think that theories and practice are separate schools of thought. Somewhere along history's timeline, a schism divided us within social justice. Each different pocket fails to respect the validity of one another and we decrease our power instead of using our respective expertise to contribute to social justice movements. These social justice movements have the possibility to build enough humility to learn from one another. Both theory and practice must be at interplay. Some theorists fail to apply their theories to the micro and macro level of their daily lives and some practitioners devalue theory. This devaluation occurs so much that theorists fail to realize that their ideological foundations are not critically theoretical nor do they resort back to those ideologies to reevaluate where their practice went astray. There has consistently been a rift between the two schools of thought that needs to cease and both schools must merge their efforts for our social justice movements to survive. Interrupting colonization of the marginalized and those who stand in solidarity with them depends on whether its roots of inequity that pervade any notions of freedom that fray from the Westernized framework of its de facto existence can be weeded out.

We can and are capable of being interconnected with theoretical intellect, mobilization, and organizing. We have to be certain of the way our theories and practices function. We must also acquire the oversight to ensure that how we as a community function does not replicate the forms of oppression that we are all too familiar with. This has been an abominable recurrence within our social justice movements wherein the marginalized marginalize their own and again bear the strange fruit of our oppressors planted seeds. In our movements are we so predisposed with the occupation of oppression and the lack of ability or willingness from antiquated models or from overall gluttony, that we have not implemented social justice theories or models that give us the opportunity to share power among ourselves. Power that extends us the opportunity to work in solidarity with those in privileged allyship for again a functional and equitable operating system. Do our systems function? Yes, but are they dysfunctional as well? The answer is without a doubt, yes. Do we want to reposition ourselves and re-examine our pure intentions of gaining power for all or do we want to rely on the applicable and winning models of power for some on a scaffolded perception of body importance and value to the society we subscribe to?

When we take a look at some past emerging social theories it becomes clear where the gaps lay in retrospect, however it is worth taking notes of the theories that have tried to fill gaps.

One being Critical Race Theory (CRT), it consistently pushes us to hold an intersectional lens and build off of the notions of racial socialization and double consciousness[305]. Critical race theory pushes and challenges our society to think in ways that allow marginalized racial groups to expand from a monolithic archetype. It allows us to find ways of not just surviving a system in different instances within society, but the theory also emphasizes the humanity and the multiplicitous identities within racially marginalized groups that were coercively migrated during this era.

Epistemology and Ontology: Foucault & Whiteness

Foucault made it exorbitantly clear that the way in which we build and sustain power is contingent on another person or social group's oppression[306]. Historically, the oppression of various different racial groups has been evident from the United States' colonization. There was, of course, slavery, exclusion acts, internment camps, patriarchal based sexual harassment and assault, gay bashing, emo-

---

[305] Bruce, Dickson D. "WEB Du Bois and the idea of double consciousness." *American Literature* 64, no. 2 (1992): 299-309.

[306] Foucault, Michel. *Power/knowledge: Selected interviews and other writings, 1972-1977.* Pantheon, 1980.

tional, mental, and physical violence, etc. These historical actions were at one time perceived to be normal. In the realm of higher education- though it may exist as a microcosm, it's "bubble" is not impermeable to social injustice. Though entry into higher education is an introduction to a more autonomous period of thought processing, our behaviors and attitudes before we get there are all informed by our lived experiences but also the history of those to whom we share identities with.

What is deemed to be normal has been structured in ways that devalue bodies that transgress from the White Anglo Saxon and Protestant (WASP) mold with the inclusion of compulsory hetero-secuality, nuclear and fiscally independent families, etc. Whiteness does not refer simply to the color of one's skin, but moreover to a state of being and an adopted lens to which one views the world from hinging on othering, power, control, colonization, and erasure. College campuses bring in a vast array of students that differ from that rubric. Yet, campuses fail to accommodate or make space for cultural differentiations or educate its public of the dominant population on what inclusion actually means[307]. Nor does the history of an oppressed people reside in spaces other than specialized electives.

The identities we hold have histories of oppression as well as privilege. Though higher education institutions claim themselves to be upper echelons of critical thinking, we are consistently affected by the way we know our bodies have been perceived and have been treated over time. More times than not, people think of higher education as a one-dimensional environment, not realizing that all of the experiences are intrinsically interconnected. We don't realize that these experiences affect the way that campus members feel in reference to safety or notions that growth is possible in that environment.

The marginalized, through their own self-determination, navigate their oppression. In 2017, there is no reason that the perpetuation of inequities and injustice should have to consistently be battled, no matter one's positionality. As time progresses, we've come to understand that the perpetuation of oppression in post-secondary spaces, formal or informal, can continue to impact society as a

---

[307] Cuyjet, Michael J., Mary F. Howard-Hamilton, and Diane L. Cooper, eds. *Multiculturalism on campus: Theory, models, and practices for understanding diversity and creating inclusion*. Stylus Publishing, LLC., 2012.

whole. At some point, amidst the ontological navigation around the oppression, people become more aware of how acutely epistemology takes its toll. Many decide to move on seeing that, society remains silent or ostensibly support "diversity and inclusion", but fall complicit to the perpetuation of these various forms of oppression itself.

When systems become complicit with the concept of whiteness, it threatens everyone marginalized by its concept. The concept of white supremacy allows space for those who have the most capital in accordance to supremacist practices to harass, brutalize, and sexually assault. Privilege gives the permission to colonize whoever and whatever one wishes, including the body and the mind.

In Nolan Leon Cabrera's [308] piece, they conducted interviews with a sample size of 12 students at a single university and the pervasiveness of whiteness is exemplified. Whiteness uses many tools to hold space and maintain power, even if it is under the guise of victimization. The sample groups created their own definitions of racism that they were familiar with or academically exposed to such as the overall topic of slavery, to which they could give no deeper understanding of. The participants interviewed also stated that they all grew up in predominantly white areas and occupy mainly white spaces at college as well. These statements give validity to the Cabrera et al. conclusion as to why the responses were what they were[309]. Responses were minimized racism because they never were in spaces with other races to be cognizant that what they say or do is actually racist. A peculiar result came of this study, that is not shocking. Many of the participants cited reverse racism as a way to orient the conversation back to the "need" for attention to be paid in the realm of how white people were being treated by the system that sought equity without acknowledgement of the oppression that allowed for their privilege.

---

[308] Cabrera, Nolan León. "Exposing Whiteness in higher education: White male college students minimizing racism, claiming victimization, and recreating White supremacy." *Race Ethnicity and Education* 17, no. 1 (2014): 30-55.

[309] Cabrera, Nolan León. "Exposing Whiteness in higher education: White male college students minimizing racism, claiming victimization, and recreating White supremacy." *Race Ethnicity and Education* 17, no. 1 (2014): 30-55.

In George Lipsitz's book[310], he explains how Whiteness as a concept translates into social spaces and how the concept of whiteness has built and strengthened through discriminatory practices, social oppression, stereotypes, and stigmas. These forms of discriminatory fuel limit access into spaces and devalues bodies that are non-white in every sector of life, from jobs, to housing, to education. The social construction of race was, as Lipsitz [311] explains, is something that has created detrimental effects for people of color on their search to live a productive life as the "distribution of wealth, prestige, and opportunity" has been inaccessible or marginally limited to people of color.[312] Lipsitz goes on to explain how white people's interest in whiteness is inarguable as they are the main beneficiary[313]. The privilege of understanding one's higher position in life as a right is only important to those who profit from it. Once power is sustained in a pocket of whiteness, it becomes easier to become complicit. It becomes easier to perpetuate, to retain power, to oppress. This ease is possible because no one wants to relinquish power that was bestowed upon them, yet they can opt into the rhetoric of meritocracy hypocritically.

Critical Race Theory Revisited

Critical Race Theory often referred to as CRT, does give credit to the idea of strides in equity, but it also focuses on their limitations or their traps. Desegregation was essentially a great stride for racial equality on the surface. However, it also extended the opportunity for the educational system to continue its trend of politically subordinating groups of color under its practice of body control and inequitable distribution and resources. The results of desegregation conjunction with redlining and the designation of taxes to particular districts recreated the same structure of inequity. This structure of inequity held less community autonomy, more opportunity to oppress through minimized social mobility, and less public education resources.

---

[310] Lipsitz, George. *The possessive investment in whiteness: How white people profit from identity politics.* Temple University Press, 2006.

[311] Lipsitz, George. *The possessive investment in whiteness: How white people profit from identity politics.* Temple University Press, 2006.

[312] Lipsitz, George. *The possessive investment in whiteness: How white people profit from identity politics.* p.11.Temple University Press, 2006.

[313] Lipsitz, George. *The possessive investment in whiteness: How white people profit from identity politics.* Temple University Press, 2006.

If education is as it claims to be, a molding of the minds, then does this institution not also bear responsibility for the racism that persists? Ignoring environmental climate and reducing a systemic and structural issue of any "-ism" is derelict at best. Critical Race Theory demands that society stop looking at racism specifically as an anecdotal phenomenon and rather one that requires our participation and complicity for its longevity.

In Gloria Ladson-Billings' piece,[314] she explores how Critical Race Theory requires that we critique legal policies that sought racial justice to understand why racism in such vast ways still persists. For the purpose of Billings' piece- she drills down into the ways by which CRT surfaces in the educational context by using her university as a testing environment by engaging in conversation with peers.

Billings [315] explains how precarious it was to even explore the issues that were connected on campus within her new university. This exemplifies how much race creates and environment of unsafety when trying to investigate its inequity at a predominantly white institution and can inform how precarious exploring any "-ism" are. Due to the difficulty of explaining how racial equity measures must be critiqued, Billings explains how storytelling is pivotal in getting people to understand the forces at play when discussing or "disguising" racism[316].

Billings states that "Our notion of race (and its use) is so complex that even when it doesn't 'make sense' we continue to employ and deploy it."[317] Billings goes on to explain that there are some terms understood to be directly correlated to whiteness (middle class, intelligence, maleness, beauty, etc.) that funnel into a concept called 'conceptual whiteness', while other terms such as (basketball

---

[314] Ladson-Billings, Gloria. "Just what is critical race theory and what's it doing in a nice field like education?." *International journal of qualitative studies in education* 11, no. 1 (1998): 7-24.

[315] Ladson-Billings, Gloria. "Just what is critical race theory and what's it doing in a nice field like education?." *International journal of qualitative studies in education* 11, no. 1 (1998): 7-24.

[316] Ladson-Billings, Gloria. "Just what is critical race theory and what's it doing in a nice field like education?." *International journal of qualitative studies in education* 11, no. 1 (1998): 8.

[317] Ladson-Billings, Gloria. "Just what is critical race theory and what's it doing in a nice field like education?." *International journal of qualitative studies in education* 11, no. 1 (1998): 8.

player, social welfare, etc.) are devalued and categorically placed into association with 'conceptual blackness'[318]

Billings also discusses the connection between law and education. Since desegregation of schools, educational institutions have been instructed to practice integration. However, historically, this implementation of policy was ignored and then coercively implemented superficially. The resistance to value different races other than whiteness, bled from social space and from one institution to another, back into social space- perfecting its cycle and its strength. Although, arguably the way that race was viewed before integration is clear in its defined and prescribed operation under segregation laws in and of itself. Even upon integration Billings points out that "curriculum is a culturally specific artifact defined to maintain a white supremacist master script"[319].

Even in higher education, understanding or learning about cultures other than glorified white history is an elective and preference and prioritization of importance is evident in the prerequisite courses (i.e. Western Civilization) needed for matriculation. As Billings[320] states "it is not just the distortions, omissions, and stereotypes of school curriculum content that must be considered. It also is the rigor of the curriculum and access to what is deemed 'enriched' curriculum via gifted and talented courses and classes that aides in this process as well.[321].

Many institutions feel that diversity creates inclusion and go no further into examining causality for low graduation rates or retention decreases. In Daniel G. Solórzano and Octavio Villalpando's piece they expand on this by stating that the mere assumption that an:

[318] Ladson-Billings, Gloria. "Just what is critical race theory and what's it doing in a nice field like education?." *International journal of qualitative studies in education* 11, no. 1 (1998): 9.
[319] Ladson-Billings, Gloria. "Just what is critical race theory and what's it doing in a nice field like education?." *International journal of qualitative studies in education* 11, no. 1 (1998): 18.
[320] Ladson-Billings, Gloria. "Just what is critical race theory and what's it doing in a nice field like education?." *International journal of qualitative studies in education* 11, no. 1 (1998): 7-24.
[321] Ladson-Billings, Gloria. "Just what is critical race theory and what's it doing in a nice field like education?." *International journal of qualitative studies in education* 11, no. 1 (1998): 18.

... increase in the absolute number or students of color in college will naturally result in the increase in the proportion of college graduates, ignores how educational systems at each point in the pipeline affect the lives of these student prior to and while in college. Moreover, this simplistic suggestion of absolute increase and proportional graduation rates minimized the extent to which policies and practices of higher education institutions help define the experiences of students of color and relieves the institution of any responsibility for influencing students' success[322].

Intersectionality

We do not exist in society as one particular identity. The reason that this text uses race as a pivot point is because it is essentially the first thing we see. Whether we assume incorrectly or not- preconceived notions based on social and historical stereotypes pervade our minds. With the concept of intersectionality, we understand that holding different identities is what creates compounded effects that equate to our fatigue[323]. For instance, one can be white and lower class- this individual experiences systemic and structural privilege along with oppression in an economic state. However, we utilize the term intersection by Crenshaw in that marginalized race is one intersection by default and this term is not applicable to white bodies because of settler colonial privilege. There are unique experiences as identities that are compounded, but the context in which intersectionality is under critical race theory. Critical race theory holds a foundation of understanding intersectionality from a marginalized race lens. To avoid playing what many have coined as

---

[322] Solorzano, Daniel G., and Octavio Villalpando. "Critical race theory, marginality, and the experience of students of color in higher education." *Sociology of education: Emerging perspectives* (1998): 21.

[323] Crenshaw, Kimberle. "Mapping the margins: Intersectionality, identity politics, and violence against women of color." *Stanford law review* (1991): 1241-1299.

Oppression Olympics presented in Yuval-Davis work [324], it is important to note that we all experience our intersections in unique ways.

As one experiences multiple marginalized identities, it becomes clear their epistemology and ontology multiplies or is compounded into one body's way of life- how they perceive themselves and how others of dominant identities will perceive them. This directly flows into not only self-efficacy but also self-determination. However intersectionality also aids in understanding how socio-political constructs have designed the level of difficulty for a person to have a higher trajectory in the different dimensions of their lives. What becomes evident is that no matter one's position, the impacts of marginalized identities and intersections thereof do not create a net of safety.

Though this section focuses much on race and the educational system in our society, some transferability is possible in that the ability to see people as multidimensional is pivotal. This section simply extends contextual examples building from the chapter on education.

Feminist Theory

It is well known that feminist theory has gone through considerable waves from the first to the fourth wave, or more commonly known to be postmodern feminism. However, as much as we want to describe feminist movements to be at the fore of social justice, it's undeniable use of exclusionary practices upholds the colonial school of thought without a doubt. The first "formal" wave of feminism could arguably be given to the suffragist movement. The right to vote for women came with many schisms such as prohibition, well-to- do women vs. women of a lower socio-economic status as well as racial exclusion and abolition[325]. The suffragist movement did involve a significant amount of strife and they did achieve victory but I suppose it depends on how we measure what the definition of victory is. The only way that the suffragist gained momentum was in making concessions to heteropatriarchal white supremacy. There was a fall out from those who wanted to include abolition and racially marginalized women's' secured right to vote in the move-

---

[324] Yuval-Davis, Nira. "Dialogical epistemology—an intersectional resistance to the "oppression Olympics"." *Gender & society* 26, no. 1 (2012): 46-54.

[325] King, Deborah K. "Multiple jeopardy, multiple consciousness: The context of a Black feminist ideology." *Signs* 14, no. 1 (1988): 42-72.

ment. Those involved in the suffragist movement that were in the minority population of the movement were told that inclusion would dilute their chance of securing what they sought for themselves. With this, we set in motion the practice of marginalization within marginalized groups to gain political power in a colonialist framework[326].

As women of color were not allowed to vote and African Americans were overall not allowed to vote, the feminist movement era moved forward with heavy critique. This social justice movement still dehumanized despite the juxtaposing rhetoric of the feminists of that time being the first wave[327]. As the second wave of feminism began to emerge, more women wanted to enter the workforce with equal pay and fight against sexual harassment, this too was exclusionary knowing that women of color still were not treated as full citizens in a de facto sense. There was also strife between those who identified as LGBTQQIA2S+ and they were excluded from this moment because they didn't want the stereotype because those in the forefront didn't want the stereotype of self-empowered white women to be equated to lesbianism because these identities were still seen as deviant[328]. It just so happens that the second wave of feminism wanted to make clear that they wanted access to the work force and equal pay. These aspirations wanted to be achieved with the expectation that those visible in the movement would be deemed a socially acceptable archetype. These archetypes were to align to "respectable" versions of femininity, and movement members were expected to agree to other social roles ascribed to them. This was yet another concession and exclusionary practice for those who did not reside within those parameters.

Once the third wave of feminism came to the fore, more women of color were completely fed up with exclusion and those who existed on the queer spectrum began to use their voices and advocate for themselves after being erased from the rhetoric of equality for so long. Many women of color, trans* bodies, and queer bodies of color began writing their own theories and participating in their own marches. This split broke off into what was called womynist

---

[326] Buechler, Steven M. *Women's movements in the United States: woman suffrage, equal rights, and beyond.* Rutgers University Press, 1990.

[327] Banks, Olive. *"Becoming a Feminist the Social Origins of" First Wave" Feminism."* (1986).

[328] Connell, Raewyn W. *"Gender and power: Society, the person and sexual politics."* John Wiley & Sons, 2014.

negating the "e" from the word. The goal was to make clear that members did not have to be built up from men or white women to actualize their efficacy. In this, those involved in the third wave of feminism sought to also push back on things that the previous feminist movements didn't talk about. Topics avoided were racism, sexual assault, ableism, reproductive justice, abortion rights, and challenged ideas of family and childcare[329]. At this time, it became clear that people were no longer accepting the colonization of their bodies or their minds. By the time the fourth or the postmodern era of feminism came to the fore, people were truly stepping into their own identity and understanding that different schools of thought could coexist as long as it did not infringe on the rights, the liberties, or the pursuit of happiness extended to others within society. Though that sounds ambiguous, it gave room for more humanization and acceptance of free expression. For those who pushed back on gender roles and those that found refuge in them to build analysis together- not of tolerance but of acceptance[330].

From feminist theory, queer theory and disability theory began to flourish[331], with the gaining momentum of free expression. The epistemology of the "closet" was beginning to be broken down aligning with the 3rd and the 4th wave of feminism. Queer theory made more room for the conversation of intersectionality and the understanding of inclusion in practice. This movement still hasn't achieved its full potential as can be seen within the LGBTQQIA2S+ movements that basically represented gay white men and white lesbians. It seems to have fallen back on the old models of exclusion. However, as more conversations stemmed from the AIDS epidemic, we started to realize that it was affecting everyone, and included conversations now in the 21st century of its impacts on women of color[332]. The issue with queer theory is that its theory couldn't keep up with its movements and scholars continue to try to capture these movements in retrospect. As social justice movements continued for the queer population, over time it excluded groups of color, groups of varying abilities, and groups with varying

[329] McCall, Leslie. "The complexity of intersectionality." Signs: Journal of women in culture and society 30, no. 3 (2005): 1771-1800.
[330] Hekman, Susan J. *Gender and knowledge: Elements of a postmodern feminism.* John Wiley & Sons, 2013.
[331] Kafer, Alison. *Feminist, queer, crip.* Indiana University Press, 2013.
[332] Quinn, Thomas C., and Julie Overbaugh. "HIV/AIDS in women: an expanding epidemic." *Science* 308, no. 5728 (2005): 1582-1583.

documentation statuses under the guise of homonormativity[333]. In time, we have gained significant strides for inclusion. Why after a century's time were we still not expanding our intellect or pragmatic practices of social justice in our rhetoric or our movements forward? Why were we still making concessions? Why did we still focus on access to oppressive systems in hopes of something as marriage? Why did this movement not also focus on and include the livability barriers that have structurally been set in place for queer populations to survive or have the sustenance level of basic needs because of social stigma?

When we think about the civil right era, we did the same thing that the feminist movements did and excluded bodies based on some notion of normalcy and the same rhetoric of "were just like you except we're black". The movement used women but did not include them i.e. Rosa Parks[334]. It used women's ideas based on fatigue but not if they weren't what society deemed as respectable, i.e. Claudette Colvin[335] . We used queer bodies' strategic planning for our social justice movement for civil rights all the while stripping them of their humanity and pushing them to the back of the line, i.e. Bayard Rustin[336]. No one told us to do that, we did it ourselves. We adopted heteropatriarchal Western framework white colonial supremacy practices and placed it on our own bodies. We made sure that we wouldn't be free just by doing that alone and in that we no longer were having land stolen or having bodies coercively migrated. We willingly gave our minds up as an offering to colonization for a piece meal of political citizenship that still hasn't been achieved.

Now we have movements such as The Movement for Black Lives and Standing Rock where the platform has shifted from the old models of exclusionary social justice. We have shifted from movement structures that entrap us between de jure law and de facto realities of social justice. Movements now are attempting to actual-

---

[333] Duggan, Lisa. "The new homonormativity: The sexual politics of neoliberalism." *Materializing democracy: Toward a revitalized cultural politics* (2002): 175-94.

[334] Perry, M. LaVora. *A History of the Civil Rights Movement.* Simon and Schuster, 2014.

[335] Perry, M. LaVora. *A History of the Civil Rights Movement.* Simon and Schuster, 2014.

[336] Perry, M. LaVora. *A History of the Civil Rights Movement. Simon and Schuster,* 2014.

ize diversification of competent allies. No longer are antiquated unjust models being used, but those in present day social justice movements are taking theory and repurposing it, building on it, and theoretically expanding these ideologies into useful forms of practice and resistance. This is what is so pivotal for this time in that we realized that these models we used before were those of our oppressors' framework and we aren't using those tools unless it is done in subterfuge or subversiveness to make it destroy itself.

Both of these movements are historically important because it brings a new approach to social justice not used before and calls for competent solidarity, multiple streams of analytical consciousness, and inclusive humanization. Movements breathing mobilization, theory, organizing, and direct action's sole purpose isn't to get people to build more political power with the system. People are trying to bring to the fore that the system never wanted them to have any political power. Movements are trying to educate its members to understand that sometimes, seats at the table within a system only use the marginalized to fuel its agenda. Evolving movements want you to see that there are ills that have not been eradicated by policy. Evolving movements want you to see that pushing people out or saying that everyone's life matters doesn't negate from the fact that people are being disproportionately impacted. Standing Rock and Water protection is not solely about political power in sovereignty. This movement is about the emphasization of sovereignty and treaties being broken. This movement is exposing imperialistic tendencies of this nation continuing to proliferate due to capitalism and, it's about the dehumanization of a people fighting for the land that belongs to them[337]. Movements are growing into something new, something with useful pieces from the past but not a direct model that could land justice work in the same cyclical form of oppression amongst the marginalized.

This is where we have reached a veering for the better, because the old models don't work and we have to keep building on our theories if we want to give ourselves any chance of liberation. We have been beaten, thrown off our land, barred access, dehumanized, had our people and cultures destroyed, and still survived. These movements are about more than surviving. They are about demanding equity, and taking our freedom. Those involved in

---

[337] Singer, Joseph William. "Canons of Conquest: The Supreme Court's Attack on Tribal Sovereignty." *New Eng. L. Rev.* 37 (2002): 641.

evolving social justice movements are also demanding humanity and embodying their initial values from start to finish. These movements are taking place within a nation state structure that could have cared less about marginalized populations after they had been disempowered structurally, disenfranchised and dispossessed[338].

Solidarity and Allyship

So what is it to be an ally; to share power? We don't have models of that working. We teach the concept of sharing within grade school but those few hours are met in contrast with a lifetime of capitalism and power gained by colonial practice. This is why sharing space or power is so difficult[339]. No one taught us how to share beyond primary years. That speaks volumes for the hypocrisy our society. That doesn't mean we can't find ways to actualize what sharing means. This is especially true, when we talk about equity and in understanding that equity calls for giving more back to the most impacted to share than on simply an equal playing field because of disenfranchisement throughout generations.

When we have conversations about solidarity and allyship it is important to consider in what ways marginalized groups have articulated the want allyship to be presented. We run into a lot of barriers when we have conversations about allyship alongside of privilege based fragility. We have to avoid savior complexes. They are not conducive to solidarity and make it clear that the deconstruction of privilege requires more education. Often when we talk about allyship and solidarity, people of privileged communities get stuck on the interpersonal level and say "I didn't do anything". If you benefit from a system that inherently marginalizes identities that you don't hold and you don't interrupt it, you are complicit. In not interrupting or dismantling oppression, you have done more damage than you realize. When I speak of competent solidarity, it means that it comes with the expectation that one educates themselves as much as possible. Competent solidarity asks that people put them-

---

[338] Omi, Michael, and Howard Winant. *Racial formation in the United States.* Routledge, 2014.

[339] Leonard, Geoffrey, and Laura Misumi. "WAIT (Why Am I Talking?): A Dialogue on Solidarity, Allyship, and Supporting the Struggle for Racial Justice without Reproducing White Supremacy." *Harvard Journal of African American Public Policy* (2016): 61.

selves in spaces (open to you) where you are the "minority" and you listen more than you talk. Solidarity expects you to take note of marginalization. It is fine to process your struggles with the willing. However, do not use your privilege to demand that someone explain their struggles within structural injustice to you and do not take up space. You can't use space with your incongruent struggles. There are places to process through privilege, and places where it's not appropriate. You can't truly understand what unique structural oppressions feel like and you never will, but you can believe someone when they tell you what a particular oppression feels like. When marginalized populations say what something makes them feel like - believe them and don't question something you never will experience.

Empathy can only go so far and allies have got to understand that. In addition, being able to take a break from social justice is a luxury. When people have to live everyday with the identities they hold especially if they cannot pass under any guise of what is considered in our society to be normal, every day is a form of resistance in spite of their barriers. Every day is a social justice movement from the moment they get out of bed to the moment they lay down to go to sleep. Navigating our own fragility comes in different ways and as stated before earlier in this text, we can occupy privilege and oppression at the same time. What is important is that our allyship is unwavering in the face of being presented with our privileges when we catch momentary social justice and historical amnesia. As stated previously, when we adopt colonial thought processes we scaffold importance of the body in alignment with its theoretical framework and its political power variance. It is important to not scaffold when we talk about solidarity but to move together and build our analysis for a stronger movement. Without this, we won't move very far, as can be seen from our previous social justice movements.

When we are in solidarity with each other one must check their whiteness, their toxic masculinity, their sexuality, their passability, and their able bodied-ness privileges. In checking that, these identities should not overshadow the most impacted. Sometimes, the approaches of calling in and calling out have been used. I myself am more of an advocate for calling in, but it takes time and does lead to exhaustion. However, calling out when time is limited leaves one to know something went wrong, but not what or why. It doesn't give time to. It doesn't give time to understand where a mistake may have lived. It doesn't set anyone up with the directions, tools, or resources and how to learn from a teachable moment. There are also instances wherein one is called out just for calling out's sake in a competition of solidarity competency. In whatever option you use- it needs to still coalesce us into a movement, it needs to be useful and productive- if it's not there's no point. I'm not saying that we need to explain everything to everyone. I do believe that one should educate themselves as much as possible- however trying to recreate a hierarchy of "I'm a better ally than you" is not useful. In addition, when spaces are held for particular identities only, do not revert back to the false validation of reverse -isms. Those spaces are set up for free thought and free processing without explaining things to people who already experience specific injustices and know its mechanisms quite well. They are setup to not have to educate, but to process, and to heal, and to rely on culturally specific practices that people don't want colonialized or turned into a spectator sport- respect that. Solidarity and allyship above anything is about respect, education, and space.

We cannot place ourselves in positions to play Oppression Olympics either when we have conversations about imminent danger or movement to mobilize for the most impacted population's safety. Again, take up space when it makes sense and at no other time. Just because a movement is giving its attention to particular bodies does not mean that yours doesn't matter. This focus means that right here, and right now a particular group's livelihood can be taken away at any minute and we have to do something. That analysis is pivotal to allyship. It's not always about you. And we have to accept that and understand truly why that is so.

Allyship and solidarity can be a challenge. Sometimes marginalized groups are experiencing their oppression so much and trying to discover ways to empower themselves that they don't have time to explain to you how they want allyship to advocacy to look for them. That's difficult for someone who is ready to help to process. But you have to just wait and interrupt in ways that you understand are, in general, acceptable forms of interruption. You can use this time to push back on irrational rationalizations in spaces that you don't want your silence to equate to complicity in. However, interruption or disruption is not the same as advocacy. Advocacy is much more personalized to those you are advocating with or on the behalf of and it's a huge responsibility that requires one to pay attention, stay educated, and understand spatiality and the impacts of it for your body and others' bodies.

Lastly, when we talk about solidarity and allyship we have to stop being so shocked and surprised while still making sure we aren't inoculated by injustice. By educating ourselves we know the predispositions of colonization that have not been interrupted. Why would you take up space to say how shocked you are? These dynamics are not new. It is understood that you can't un-know what you have been exposed to. But when it's like a new world is being shown to you and you still want to see beauty in it, it displaces focus away from injustice. That's not to say beauty doesn't exist, but don't be shocked by continuous modus operandi, do what you can to help shift it.

In conclusion, understand that justice is never done- a march does not make you an ally for life. It just doesn't. This nation is surreptitious and finds new ways to oppress bodies every single day. Though one should take solace in being a part of something greater than themselves. There are no cookies extended for demanding that people be treated like human beings in an equitable way. You stand in solidarity as an ally because you care, nothing more and nothing less- no incentives, just justice. And knowing the ways that colonialism and meritocracy operates, we expect to be congratulated for doing "nice" things but justice isn't about nice things. These social justice movements are about getting free. The reward comes when all of us have and can hold liberation in our lives. No matter how much terms, theories, and expectations shift, stay invested. No matter how difficult allyship or solidarity may be at times, it's better than falling back into our spaces of privilege and dwelling there watching the same cyclical oppression. This is an oppression that continues to destroy our humanity as we watch the show and that we thought our non-negotiables of seeking self-determination for all were.

Chapter 6

Trauma

Socialization

Those who have marginalized identities are socialized to, for lack of a better term, "learn how to get along, to get along". But in that, we are socialized on ways to navigate through injustice but to not empower ourselves or eradicate the injustices we face for us and future generations. We often operate in stealth to survive in various forms and in doing so, we become acutely aware of our otherness and the ranking of our bodies as less than[340]. Society in the United States context has made it just within an inch of intolerability to exist within its borders. This takes its toll. For some time, we have called this navigation and lessons of what our body means in society as marginalized socialization. This socialization impacts multiple generations at a time, as we are socialized in ways that keep us alive, but don't build our efficacy and don't ensure our full safety. It is understood how preceding generations would push for this socialization, but where it landed us was in a place of subservience in public space and in our private lives However, we are never allowed to be our full selves, and feel the need to assimilate to gain minimal access to public spaces and institutions[341].

Privileged bodies are not safe from the ills of socialization however. Those that hold historically valued identities within society often times are socialized to not be aware of their privilege and to hold or maintain the status quo of inequity with a system they have been told is normal. In that, the insidious seed of colonization are once again planted and take hold in strong roots intergenerationally. Privileged groups continue to write the normative narrative of our society, not understanding that assimilation is a concession that marginalized groups do to have a chance at systemic access. This

---

[340] Comas-Díaz, Lillian. "Racial trauma recovery: A race-informed therapeutic approach to racial wounds." (2016).

[341] Linder, Chris, and Katrina L. Rodriguez. "Learning from the experiences of self-identified women of color activists." *Journal of College Student Development* 53, no. 3 (2012): 383-398.

has caused more detriment overall than success. Being alive is not the same thing as living and at this point in time, if we can't live, then how much power is in being alive? We have to disrupt the socialization for the marginalized and make clear to those with privilege identities that multiple streams of consciousness have been held because of historical and present day injustice. This illumination needs to be brought to society's attention so people can stop believing that their perceptions are the baseline of normalities, but moreover, that hegemony allowed for them to hold the pen to the narrative.

Multiple Streams of Consciousness

In understanding multiple streams of consciousness, we branch off from the concept of double consciousness and expand on it in an inclusive manner to make way for gender, sexuality, ability, and race, documentation, etc. We understand that there are different experiences that those with varying intersections have. For those with identity intersections, we compound each stream of consciousness. The socialized navigation among many identities exists in the ontology of how one sole person lives their lives[342]. That's a lot of frameworks at play at the same time, and to think it doesn't take its toll is remiss. Operating on multiple streams of consciousness calls for us to adjust our impression management and how we show up in a room. This depends on how much our bodies transgress from predominantly presented bodies and how much we have to assimilate for access into that space.

We are constantly trying to maintain knowledge of who we are without internalizing our oppression as well as navigating through it. It leads to an unimaginable amount of fatigue. It could be said by the ignorant- that no one told us to do this. One arrives to that conclusion without understanding that you do what you have to do in a system that is ok with seeing you starve and be abused literally and systemically. In the next section, we'll be talking about racial battle fatigue, but some of its principles are again transferable to the overall conversation of fatigue for the marginalized. We're essentially exhausted and exasperated and as continued conversations come

---

[342] Harris, Tina M. "Black feminist thought and cultural contracts: Understanding the intersection and negotiation of racial, gendered, and professional identities in the academy." *New Directions for Teaching and Learning* 2007, no. 110 (2007): 55-64.

to the fore about social justice, sometimes we're too busy experiencing oppression to fight it.

Racial Battle Fatigue

Racial Battle fatigue discusses the way in which racial minorities, through navigating whiteness in society, have grown exhausted. The term emphasizes that marginalized races are experiencing far more than what can be reduced to "tiredness". As social aspects of life continue to marginalize, marginalized populations have continued living in a society where their overall wellbeing is at risk despite policy amendments and social justice movements. Policy implementation has not worked, because people's minds around the concept of power and stereotype buy-in have not shifted. Many are fatigued and now simply ask- what now?

In William A. Smith [343] book, Williams begins his paper with a quote from a senior black male professor:

If you can think of the mind as having 100 ergs of energy, and the average man uses 50 percent of this energy dealing with everyday problems of the world- just general kinds of things- then he has 50 percent more to do creative kinds of things that he wants to do. Now, that's a white person. Now a black person also has 100 ergs. He has 50 percent the same way a white man does, dealing with what the white man has [to deal with], so he has 50 percent left? But he uses 25 percent fighting being black, [with] all the problems being Black and what it means [344].

---

[343] Smith, William A. "Black faculty coping with racial battle fatigue: The campus racial climate in a post-civil rights era." *A long way to go: Conversations about race by African American faculty and graduate students* 14 (2004): 171-190.

[344] Smith, William A. "Black faculty coping with racial battle fatigue: The campus racial climate in a post-civil rights era." *A long way to go: Conversations about race by African American faculty and graduate students* 14 (2004).

Smith[345] also goes on to explain how a historian for education presented an endeavor pushed by the Julius Rosenwald Fund post World War II. This initiative sought to urge approximately 600 universities to consider hiring qualified African American scholars. The result of this study was not an acknowledgement that something went awry in hiring and equity processes. The response was one that was aghast at the "special" effort based suggestion to "discriminate against whites" [346]. Equity processes were seen as a threat. The response completely ignored the institutions historical common practice to exclude African Americans altogether and positioned those who privileged most from injustice, as victims.

Racist ideologies and stereotypes like these have persisted into present times and are the sources of many decisions whites and other non-blacks make in assessing their disdain, relationships with, acceptance of, and intimacy with and toward African Americans. In understanding how fatigue has not spun into eventual collapse Smith[347] explains that "the most defensible answer is found in proactive and protective cultural strengths that African American parents teach their children, a concept coined racial socialization"[348].

In Christine Sleeter's work[349], she states that "White people do not talk about race or racism. Instead we walk about group differences, very often in ways that simplify and devalue others while rendering Whiteness itself as invisible or normal"[350]. Smith explains that "Ra-

---

[345] Sleeter, Christine E. "How white teachers construct race." *The Routledge-Falmer reader in multicultural education* (2004): 163-178.

[346] Smith, William A. "Black faculty coping with racial battle fatigue: The campus racial climate in a post-civil rights era." *A long way to go: Conversations about race by African American faculty and graduate students* 14 (2004): 173.

[347] Smith, William A. "Black faculty coping with racial battle fatigue: The campus racial climate in a post-civil rights era." *A long way to go: Conversations about race by African American faculty and graduate students* 14 (2004): 171.

[348] Smith, William A. "Black faculty coping with racial battle fatigue: The campus racial climate in a post-civil rights era." *A long way to go: Conversations about race by African American faculty and graduate students* 14 (2004): 183.

[349] Sleeter, Christine E. "How white teachers construct race." *The Routledge-Falmer reader in multicultural education* (2004): 163-178.

[350] Sleeter, Christine E. "How white teachers construct race." *The Routledge-Falmer reader in multicultural education* (2004): 176.

cial stereotypes and prejudice become useful explanations, for White college students, about why Blacks do not have as much nor do as well as whites in several areas of society" [351].

Mental Health and the Monolith

When we talk about all the things that marginalized bodies have experienced, why we feel that this fatigue and these injustices don't take a mental toll is unfathomable. However, we rarely allow marginalized bodies to exist multidimensionally or in any form beyond a monolith. Social forces take a tremendous taxing toll on a body and it has always affected the mental health of us all. This section expounds on social forces of mental health and not necessarily preexisting mental illnesses.

This conversation is more so about the compounded effect of social forces and experiences that lead us to realizing that we have gone through "-isms". Those forces and those experiences have traumatized us in the ways we process things, experience, capitulate to, avoid, opt-in, or opt out of particular social functions and dynamics. We often reduce and minimize "-isms" and let it seem as if they operate on their own and are intangible. However, for every action there is a reaction. The reaction to "-isms" are different forms of trauma. Someone getting sexually assaulted, gay bashed, harassed for being transgender, being threatened with deportation, etc., impacts who share identities with those attacked. Some have their spaces encroached upon because of their disability and are made fun of in social spaces, and it induces trauma. We can't just get over it, it's not that simple because its recurring, systemically accepted, and structurally supported. This trauma is carried with us especially if we are not given spaces to articulate and processes through our experiences to realize how our own trauma from these "-isms" have impacted and directed our lives. If we don't have the conversation, we won't be able to take our power back.

---

[351] Sleeter, Christine E. "How white teachers construct race." *The Routledge-Falmer reader in multicultural education* (2004): 178.

Self-Care and Healing

Now we have taken more time to create self-care and healing spaces and offer a sense of community in different ways that allow us to take care of ourselves. However, the distinction must be made that because of the impact of colonization of land, of bodies, of history, and of minds, this is no simple feat. Self-care are tools of stepping back, focusing and centering on the needs that we as individuals must make sure that we are able to get through life on a day by day basis. Self-care doesn't hinge on resilience in pushing through, but on equipping ourselves with ways and practices to not cope with injustice but to help us move forward while still maintaining our resolve and self-efficacy[352]. These stepping stones of self-care aid in healing. Healing is a larger process and conversation in trying to find ways to heal individually, as community, intersectionally, and intergenerationally. The past and the present impacts of oppression have to be addressed meaningfully so that we can move forward with designing our liberation and move towards it by healing our roots.

Healing requires unpacking and deconstruction not only the intentions of colonization, but how it infiltrated our communities. Healing also helps us go back and get what was rightfully ours and that's our own stories, our own efficacy, our own culture, and our own self-empowerment. We have to heal the wounds we've been struck with whether our oppressors realize the knife is in our backs or not. We have to heal ourselves and it takes time, and trial and error. It's not always going to work but trying shows our grit and our resilience. Having a way to heal from the trauma placed on our bodies and our minds are the only ways to start internally and collectively deconstructing the damage that has been done to us so that we can recreate ourselves. So that we can recreate ourselves without letting colonization that traumatized us lead our narrative.

---

[352] Hardy, Kenneth V. "Healing the hidden wounds of racial trauma." *Reclaiming Children and Youth* 22, no. 1 (2013): 24.

Articulating Trauma

As stated before, we as a community have spent a lot of time just surviving, but it is important to name trauma for what it is instead of reducing it for ourselves as "sad" or "tired"[353]. It's more than that and getting people to understand how deep the trauma of colonization goes beyond simple articulation. This is just the starting part. Colonization directly impacts the marginalized in ways that need to be absorbed, understood, respected, and given space. Those who experience trauma go through the process of healing themselves for them and their community so that fatigue doesn't always have to be our story, so that colonization does not write our story. This is also necessary so that we can have the energy to write our own story instead of finding maladaptive ways to "get along to get along", or consistently having to "make a way out of no way". It's time we make our own way".

---

[353] McGee, Ebony O., and David Stovall. "Reimagining Critical Race Theory in Education: Mental Health, Healing, and the Pathway to Liberatory Praxis." *Educational Theory* 65, no. 5 (2015): 491-511.

Chapter 7

Epilogue: Creating Ourselves

James Baldwin said that "our crown has already been bought and paid for. All we have to do is wear it". What would it mean if we behaved like that? Not in that colonial predisposed meaning of what a crown means by way of ruling over other people, but with understanding. Understanding that the pain, the blood and tears shed have not been all for naught and that we don't need permission from a system of oppression to actualize our freedom.

What if we walked through the days with and as our full selves.

As if we were aware of the authority that we hold over our own bodies?

What would that take, to be the rulers of our movement, thought, speech, expression, our minds?

I think we are at a point where we can't afford to be complicit anymore. We can't be the strange fruit and hang ourselves or be hanged from trees. I'd rather die free than live a slave.

However, to empower the marginalized we must discuss the structural and cultural differences that have marginalized us and emphasize the cultural efficacy of a marginalized people.

It is simple to say let's just all be people, but the foundation of colonialism exists within a bias that has become automated and requires deconstruction. Colonialism of the mind pits us against one another as its destruction carries on without interruption due to our arbitrary distractions of relative deprivation and pointless competition.

It must be articulated that, just because I suggest we become innovative, create what we think our own freedom and self-autonomy could be, it does not mean we exist as if our oppression is not real.

We however, are aware of our stories, and we should share them, learn from them, be guided by them. Instead of imploring that someone who doesn't want to understand try to when you don't need them to get you and your experience to be liberated.

Go back and get you and those who encourage self-care and collective healing from trauma.

And for bodies that benefit from historical privilege-

When one asks, "when will we be done paying for the sins of our fathers"- it depends on when you consistently and sustainably stop benefitting from their oppression and share power. When you're willing to begin again, when you're willing to deconstruct and take bricks away from walls of barred access, and until self-empowerment does not threaten you.

We cannot behave as if fixing where we are, is an easily achieved thing.

When we have the discussion of creating ourselves, it is with the *a priori* that we were never given the chance to truly create ourselves in the first place. We are bound by colonialism and what we have to do is figure out alternative ways to untie ourselves without using the same tools that bound us and encouraged us to bind each other.

Our freedom cannot be contingent on anyone else's oppression just because it's the practice we are most familiar with.

To find true definitions of what "free" is, it can't be defined by what defined us in shackles. We must create our own definitions, our own models, our own thought, our own practice. We must take these definitions and include our entire community and not just parts of us, the whole of the marginalized.

We must walk as if we own ourselves.

That's not to say that our blood and tears won't be shed, that we will prevail unscathed.

Walk with heads held high understanding that the systems seeks to oppress us, but demanding too, the space to create ourselves. Stepping into our own glory of humanization is necessary.

What if we behaved as if we were free until we actually were through our own unwillingness to bend? Our unwillingness to be broken-in.

The interesting point of understanding ourselves is in the time and space it takes to achieve metacognition and be aware of our thought processes.

The very space we can inhabit of understanding our oppression while also moving forward through life actualizing our own semantic degrees of freedom transcends us.

The neurocognition of our connections and corresponding actions dictate the trajectory of our lives. With interruption there can be space to develop alchemy of the mind and redefine ourselves while still understanding the past indiscretions of injustice that have planted its malignant seeds.

There are opportunities to disrupt the harvest of our young minds and become agriculturalists of our own nourishment rather than slaves of a stolen land and a manufactured world we were never considered to be good enough for.

Create anew.

Everything.

Bibliography

Adams, David Wallace. Education for Extinction: American Indians and the Boarding School Experience, 1875-1928. University Press of Kansas, 2501 W. 15th St., Lawrence, KS 66049, 1995.

Aggarwal, Arjun P., and M. Gupta. "Sexual harassment in the workplace." Editorial Board (2000): 16.

Ainslie, Ricardo C. "Cultural mourning, immigration, and engagement: Vignettes from the Mexican experience." The New Immigrant in American Society: Interdisciplinary Perspectives on the New Immigration 355 (2014).

Alba, Richard, and Victor Nee. Remaking the American mainstream: Assimilation and contemporary immigration. Harvard University Press, 2009.

Alexander, Michelle. "The New Jim Crow." Ohio St. J. Crim. L. 9 (2011): 7.

Alexander, Michelle. The new Jim Crow: Mass incarceration in the age of colorblindness. The New Press, 2012.

Alsultany, Evelyn. Arabs and Muslims in the Media: Race and Representation after 9/11. nyu Press, 2012.

Amott, Teresa L., and Julie A. Matthaei. Race, gender, and work: A multi-cultural economic history of women in the United States. South End Press, 1996.

Arbona, Consuelo, Norma Olvera, Nestor Rodriguez, Jacqueline Hagan, Adriana Linares, and Margit Wiesner. "Acculturative stress among documented and undocumented Latino immigrants in the United States." Hispanic Journal of Behavioral Sciences 32, no. 3 (2010): 362-384.

Arvin, Maile, Eve Tuck, and Angie Morrill. "Decolonizing feminism: Challenging connections between settler colonialism and heteropatriarchy." Feminist Formations 25, no. 1 (2013): 8-34.

Awad, Germine H. "The impact of acculturation and religious identification on perceived discrimination for Arab/Middle Eastern Americans." Cultural Diversity and Ethnic Minority Psychology 16, no. 1 (2010): 59.

Bailey, Alison. "Strategic ignorance." Race and epistemologies of ignorance (2007): 77-94.

Baker, Paula. "The domestication of politics: Women and American political society, 1780-1920." The American Historical Review 89, no. 3 (1984): 620-647.

Banks, Olive. "Becoming a Feminist the Social Origins of" First Wave" Feminism." (1986).

Bartholet, Elizabeth. "Proof of Discriminatory Intent Under Title VII: United States Postal Service Board of Governors v. Aikens." California Law Review 70, no. 5 (1982): 1201-1220.

Bartky, Sandra Lee. Femininity and domination: Studies in the phenomenology of oppression. Psychology Press, 1990.

Baynton, Douglas C. "Disability and the justification of inequality in American history." The disability studies reader 17 (2013): 33-57.

Becker, Gary S. "Human capital revisited." In Human Capital: A Theoretical and Empirical Analysis with Special Reference to Education (3rd Edition), pp. 15-28. The University of Chicago Press, 1994.

Beemyn, Brett Genny, Andrea Domingue, Jessica Pettitt, and Todd Smith. "Suggested steps to make campuses more trans-inclusive." Journal of gay & lesbian issues in education 3, no. 1 (2005): 89-94.

Behan, Cormac. "Learning to escape: Prison education, rehabilitation and the potential for transformation." Journal of Prison Education and Reentry 1, no. 1 (2014): 20-31.

Bell Jr, Derrick A. "Brown v. Board of Education and the interest-convergence dilemma." Harvard Law Review (1980): 518-533.

Bernasconi, Robert. "On needing not to know and forgetting what one never knew: The epistemology of ignorance in Fanon's critique of Sartre." Sullivan and Tuana, Race and Epistemologies of Ignorance (2007): 231-38.

Berry, Wendell. The unsettling of America: Culture & agriculture. Counterpoint, 2015.

Bhagwati, Jagdish. "Borders beyond control." Foreign Aff. 82 (2003): 98.

Bhattacharyya, Gargi S. Dangerous brown men: exploiting sex, violence and feminism in the 'war on terror'. Zed, 2008.

Blackhawk, Ned. Violence over the land: Indians and empires in the early American West. Harvard University Press, 2009.

Blevins, Jeffrey Layne. "Counter-hegemonic media: Can cyberspace resist corporate colonization." Cyberimperialism?: Global Relations in the New Electronic Frontier (2001): 140-151.

Blumrosen, Ruth G. "Wage Discrimination, Job Segregation, and the Title VII of the Civil Rights Act of 1964." U. Mich. JL Reform 12 (1978): 397.

Bourdieu, Pierre. "The forms of capital.(1986)." Cultural theory: An anthology (2011): 81-93.

Boustan, Leah, Fernando Ferreira, Hernan Winkler, and Eric M. Zolt. "The effect of rising income inequality on taxation and public expenditures: Evidence from US municipalities and school districts, 1970–2000." Review of Economics and Statistics 95, no. 4 (2013): 1291-1302.

Bruce, Dickson D. "WEB Du Bois and the idea of double consciousness." American Literature 64, no. 2 (1992): 299-309.

Buechler, Steven M. Women's movements in the United States: woman suffrage, equal rights, and beyond. Rutgers University Press, 1990.

Bunten, Alexis Celeste. "Sharing culture or selling out? Developing the commodified persona in the heritage industry." American Ethnologist 35, no. 3 (2008): 380-395.

Bush, George W. The national security strategy of the United States of America. EXECUTIVE OFFICE OF THE PRESIDENT WASHINGTON DC, 2002.

Cabrera, Nolan León. "Exposing Whiteness in higher education: White male college students minimizing racism, claiming victimization, and recreating White supremacy." Race Ethnicity and Education 17, no. 1 (2014): 30-55.

Caouette, Julie, and Donald M. Taylor. "Don't blame me for what my ancestors did. "In Revisiting The Great White North?, pp. 89-104. Sense Publishers, 2015.

Chafe, William Henry. The Unfinished Journey: America Since World War II. Oxford University Press, USA, 2003.

Christensen, Linda. "Rethinking Research: Reading and Writing about the Roots of Gentrification." English Journal 105, no. 2 (2015): 15.

Churchill, Ward. "Indians are us? Culture and genocide in Native North America." (1994).

Clark, Kenneth B. Dark ghetto: Dilemmas of social power. Wesleyan University Press, 1989.

Coate, Stephen, and Glenn C. Loury. "Will affirmative-action policies eliminate negative stereotypes?." The American Economic Review (1993): 1220-1240.

Cobas, José A., Jorge Duany, and Joe R. Feagin. How the United States racializes Latinos: White hegemony and its consequences. Routledge, 2015.

Cockburn, Cynthia. In the way of women: Men's resistance to sex equality in organizations. No. 18. Cornell University Press, 1991.

Cole, David, and James X. Dempsey. Terrorism and the constitution: Sacrificing civil liberties in the name of national security. The New Press, 2006.

Cole, David. No equal justice: Race and class in the American criminal justice system. The New Press, 1999.

Collins, Patricia Hill. "It's all in the family: Intersections of gender, race, and nation." Hypatia 13, no. 3 (1998): 62-82.

Comas-Díaz, Lillian. "Racial trauma recovery: A race-informed therapeutic approach to racial wounds." (2016).

Congress, By. "Chinese Exclusion Act." In 47th Congress, Session I. 1882.

Connell, Raewyn W. Gender and power: Society, the person and sexual politics. John Wiley & Sons, 2014.

Copenhaver-Johnson, Jeane F., Joy T. Bowman, and Angela C. Johnson. "Santa stories: Children's inquiry about race during picture-book read-alouds." Language Arts 84, no. 3 (2007): 234-244.

Corrigan, Patrick, Fred E. Markowitz, Amy Watson, David Rowan, and Mary Ann Kubiak. "An attribution model of public discrimination towards persons with mental illness." Journal of health and Social Behavior (2003): 162-179.

Cotter, Anne-Marie Mooney. Culture clash: an international legal perspective on ethnic discrimination. Routledge, 2016.

Crawford, Elizabeth. The Women's Suffrage Movement: A Reference Guide 1866-1928. Routledge, 2003.

Crenshaw, Kimberle Williams. "Race, reform, and retrenchment: Transformation and legitimation in antidiscrimination law." Harvard Law Review (1988): 1331-1387.

Crenshaw, Kimberle. "Demarginalizing the intersection of race and sex: A black feminist critique of antidiscrimination doctrine, feminist theory and antiracist politics." U. Chi. Legal F. (1989): 139.

Crenshaw, Kimberle. "Mapping the margins: Intersectionality, identity politics, and violence against women of color." Stanford law review (1991): 1241-1299.

Cross, Ian. "Music, cognition, culture, and evolution." Annals of the New York Academy of sciences 930, no. 1 (2001): 28-42.

Curtin, Nicola, Anna Kende, and Judit Kende. "Navigating multiple identities: The simultaneous influence of advantaged and disadvantaged identities on politicization and activism." Journal of Social Issues 72, no. 2 (2016): 264-285.

Curtis, Michael Kent. "A Unique Religious Exemption from Antidiscrimination Laws in the Case of Gays? Putting the Call for Exemptions for Those Who Discriminate Against Married or Marrying Gays in Context." In The Rule of Law and the Rule of God, pp. 83-114. Palgrave Macmillan US, 2014.

Cuyjet, Michael J., Mary F. Howard-Hamilton, and Diane L. Cooper, eds. Multiculturalism on campus: Theory, models, and practices for understanding diversity and creating inclusion. Stylus Publishing, LLC., 2012.

Daniels, Roger. Asian America: Chinese and Japanese in the United States since 1850. University of Washington Press, 2011.

Daniels, Roger. Prisoners Without Trial: Japanese Americans in World War II. Macmillan, 2004.

Daniels, Vera I. "Minority Students in Gifted and Special Education Programs The Case for Educational Equity." The Journal of Special Education 32, no. 1 (1998): 41-43.

Davidson, Chandler. Quiet revolution in the South: The impact of the Voting Rights Act, 1965-1990. Princeton University Press, 1994.

Davis, Angela Y. The meaning of freedom: And other difficult dialogues. City Lights Books, 2013.

Dawson, Hannah. "Do they look like me?: Rethinking representation and its relationship with freedom." Juncture 21, no. 2 (2014): 136-139.

Dear, Michael. "Understanding and overcoming the NIMBY syndrome." Journal of the American Planning Association 58, no. 3 (1992): 288-300.

Dewey, John, and Melvin L. Rogers. The public and its problems: An essay in political inquiry. Penn State Press, 2012.

DiAngelo, Robin. "White fragility." The International Journal of Critical Pedagogy 3, no. 3 (2011).

Dixon, Travis L., and Daniel Linz. "Race and the misrepresentation of victimization on local television news." Communication Research 27, no. 5 (2000): 547-573.

Du Bois, William Edward Burghardt. The talented tenth. James Pott and Company, 1903.

Duckworth, Angela Lee, and Patrick D. Quinn. "Development and validation of the Short Grit Scale (GRIT–S)." Journal of personality assessment 91, no. 2 (2009): 166-174.

Duggan, Lisa. "The new homonormativity: The sexual politics of neoliberalism." Materializing democracy: Toward a revitalized cultural politics (2002): 175-94.

Dumont, Louis. Homo hierarchicus: The caste system and its implications. University of Chicago Press, 1980.

Earle, Chris S. "Dispossessed: Prisoner Response-Ability and Resistance at the Limits of Subjectivity." Rhetoric Society Quarterly 46, no. 1 (2016): 47-65.

Earley, P. Christopher. "Self or group? Cultural effects of training on self-efficacy and performance." Administrative Science Quarterly (1994): 89-117.

Eccles, Jacquelynne S. "Gender roles and women's achievement-related decisions." Psychology of women Quarterly 11, no. 2 (1987): 135-172.

Epstein, Barbara Leslie. "The Politics of Domesticity Women, Evangelism, and Temperance in Nineteenth-Century America." (1981).

Evans, David. Sexual citizenship: The material construction of sexualities. Routledge, 2013.

Feagin, Joe R. The new urban paradigm: Critical perspectives on the city. Rowman & Littlefield, 1998.

Feagin, Joe. Systemic racism: A theory of oppression. Routledge, 2013.

Ferber, Abby L. "The culture of privilege: Color-blindness, postfeminism, and christonormativity." Journal of Social Issues 68, no. 1 (2012): 63-77.

Fernandez, Luis A., and Laura Huey. "Is resistance futile? Thoughts on resisting surveillance." Surveillance & Society 6, no. 3 (2009): 199-202.

Fields, Barbara Jeanne. "Slavery, race and ideology in the United States of America." New Left Review 181 (1990): 95.

Fishel, Andrew, and Janice Pottker. "National Politics and Sex Discrimination in Education." (1977).

Fisher, Linda E. "Guilt by expressive association: Political profiling, surveillance and the privacy of groups." Ariz. L. Rev. 46 (2004): 621.

Fitzgerald, Kathleen J. "A Sociology of Race/Ethnicity Textbooks: Avoiding White Privilege, Ahistoricism, and Use of the Passive Voice." Sociological Focus 45, no. 4 (2012): 338-357.

Fleisher, Martin. "The ways of Machiavelli and the ways of politics." History of Political Thought 16, no. 3 (1995): 330-355.

Fletcher, Laurel E., and Harvey M. Weinstein. "Violence and social repair: Rethinking the contribution of justice to reconciliation." Human Rights Quarterly 24, no. 3 (2002): 573-639.

Foley, Michael S. Confronting the war machine: Draft resistance during the Vietnam War. Univ of North Carolina Press, 2003.

Foss, Sonja K., Mary E. Domenico, and Karen A. Foss. Gender stories: Negotiating identity in a binary world. Waveland Press, 2012.

Foucault, Michel. Power/knowledge: Selected interviews and other writings, 1972-1977. Pantheon, 1980.

Fox-Genovese, Elizabeth. Within the plantation household: Black and white women of the old south. UNC Press Books, 2000.

Freelon, Deen Goodwin, Charlton D. McIlwain, and Meredith D. Clark. "Beyond the hashtags:# Ferguson,# Blacklivesmatter, and the online struggle for offline justice." Available at SSRN (2016).

Freire, Paulo, and Donaldo Macedo. "A dialogue: Culture, language, and race." Harvard Educational Review 65, no. 3 (1995): 377-403.

Furnivall, John Sydenham. Colonial policy and practice. Cambridge University Press, 2014.

Furth-Matzkin, Meirav, and Cass R. Sunstein. "Social Influences on Policy Preferences: Conformity and Reactance." (2016).

Gagliardone, Iginio, Danit Gal, Thiago Alves, and Gabriela Martinez. Countering online hate speech. UNESCO Publishing, 2015.

Garrison, Mark J. A measure of failure: The political origins of standardized testing. SUNY Press, 2009.

Garza, Alicia. "A herstory of the# blacklivesmatter movement." (2014).

Gay, Geneva. "Culturally responsive teaching in special education for ethnically diverse students: Setting the stage." International Journal of Qualitative Studies in Education 15, no. 6 (2002): 613-629.

Ghaill, Mac An. The making of men: Masculinities, sexualities and schooling. McGraw-Hill Education (UK), 1994.

Gines, Kathryn T. "6. Arendt's Violence/Power Distinction and Sartre's Violence/Counter-Violence Distinction: The Phenomenology of Violence in Colonial and Post-Colonial

Context." In Phenomenologies of Violence, pp. 123-144. Brill, 2013.

Giroux, Henry A. Twilight of the Social: Resurgent Politics in an Age of Disposability. Routledge, 2015.

Greene, David. "Gatekeepers: the role of adult education practitioners and programs in social control." Journal for Critical Education Policy Studies 5, no. 2 (2007): 411-437.

Greenwood, Ronni Michelle. "Remembrance, responsibility, and reparations: The use of emotions in talk about the 1921 Tulsa Race Riot." Journal of Social Issues 71, no. 2 (2015): 338-355.

Greer, Chris. "Crime and media: understanding the connections." Criminology 2 (2009): 177-203.

Guelzo, Allen C. Lincoln's Emancipation Proclamation: The End of Slavery in America. Simon and Schuster, 2005.

Gupta, Monisha Das. Unruly immigrants: Rights, activism, and transnational South Asian politics in the United States. Duke University Press, 2006.

Haller, John S. Outcasts from evolution: Scientific attitudes of racial inferiority, 1859-1900. SIU Press, 1971.

Ham, Ken, A. Charles Ware, and Todd A. Hillard. Darwin's Plantation: Evolution's Racist Roots. Master Books, 2007.

Haney-López, Ian. Dog whistle politics: How coded racial appeals have reinvented racism and wrecked the middle class. Oxford University Press, 2015.

Hardy, Kenneth V. "Healing the hidden wounds of racial trauma." Reclaiming Children and Youth 22, no. 1 (2013): 24.

Harnois, Catherine E. "Jeopardy, Consciousness, and Multiple Discrimination: Intersecting Inequalities in Contemporary Western Europe." In Sociological Forum, vol. 30, no. 4, pp. 971-994. 2015.

Harper, Phillip Brian. "Passing for what? Racial masquerade and the demands of upward mobility." Callaloo 21, no. 2 (1998): 381-397.

Harris, Fredrick C. "The rise of respectability politics." Dissent 61, no. 1 (2014): 33-37.

Harris, Tina M. "Black feminist thought and cultural contracts: Understanding the intersection and negotiation of racial, gendered, and professional identities in the academy." New Directions for Teaching and Learning 2007, no. 110 (2007): 55-64.

Harvey, Mary R. "Towards an ecological understanding of resilience in trauma survivors: Implications for theory, research, and practice." Journal of Aggression, Maltreatment & Trauma 14, no. 1-2 (2007): 9-32.

Haymes, Stephen Nathan. Race, culture, and the city: A pedagogy for Black urban struggle. SUNY Press, 1995.

Heale, Michael J. McCarthy's Americans: red scare politics in state and nation, 1935-1965. University of Georgia Press, 1998.

Hekman, Susan J. Gender and knowledge: Elements of a postmodern feminism. John Wiley & Sons, 2013.

Hodson, Gordon, and Malvina N. Skorska. "Tapping generalized essentialism to predict outgroup prejudices." British Journal of Social Psychology 54, no. 2 (2015): 371-382.

Hogg, Michael A. "Intergroup relations." In Handbook of social psychology, pp. 533-561. Springer Netherlands, 2013.

Holiday, Billie. Strange Fruit

Hudson, Barbara, and Barbara Hudson, eds. Race, crime and justice. Aldershot: Dartmouth, 1996.

Hughes, Diane, James Rodriguez, Emilie P. Smith, Deborah J. Johnson, Howard C. Stevenson, and Paul Spicer. "Parents' ethnic-racial socialization practices: a review of research and directions for future study." Developmental psychology 42, no. 5 (2006): 747.

Hummel, Jeffrey. Emancipating slaves, enslaving free men: a history of the American civil war. Open court, 2013.

Hutchinson, Sikivu. "Whose Bodies? Black Lives Matter and the Reproductive Justice Imperative." The Humanist 76, no. 3 (2016): 10. Ignatiev, Noel. How the Irish became white. Routledge, 2009

Inglehart, Ronald. The silent revolution: Changing values and political styles among Western publics. Princeton University Press, 2015.

Ingstad, Benedicte. "The disabled person in the community: social and cultural aspects."

International journal of rehabilitation research 13, no. 3 (1990): 187.

Ivey, Allen E., and Carlos P. Zalaquett. "In the Special Issue on Social Justice Leadership." Journal for Social Action in Counseling and Psychology 3, no. 1 (2011): 102.

James, Lois, Stephen M. James, and Bryan J. Vila. "The Reverse Racism Effect." Criminology & Public Policy (2016).

Jones, Maxine D. "The Rosewood Massacre and the Women Who Survived It." The Florida Historical Quarterly 76, no. 2 (1997): 193-208.

Kafer, Alison. Feminist, queer, crip. Indiana University Press, 2013.

Kalhan, Anil. "Rethinking immigration detention." Colum. L. Rev. Sidebar 110 (2010): 42.

Katznelson, Ira. When affirmative action was white: An untold history of racial inequality in twentieth-century America. WW Norton & Company, 2005.

Kellner, Douglas, and Jeff Share. "Toward critical media literacy: Core concepts, debates, organizations, and policy." Discourse:

studies in the cultural politics of education 26, no. 3 (2005): 369-386.

Kellner, Douglas. Media culture: Cultural studies, identity and politics between the modern and the post-modern. Routledge, 2003.

Kerr, Audrey Elisa. The Paper Bag Principle: Class, colorism, and rumor and the case of Black Washington. Univ. of Tennessee Press, 2006.

Kim, Catherine Y., Daniel J. Losen, and Damon T. Hewitt. The school-to-prison pipeline: Structuring legal reform. NYU Press, 2010.

Kincheloe, Joe L., Shirley R. Steinberg, Nelson M. Rodriguez, and Ronald E. Chennault, eds. White reign: Deploying whiteness in America. Palgrave Macmillan, 2000.

King, Deborah K. "Multiple jeopardy, multiple consciousness: The context of a Black feminist ideology." Signs 14, no. 1 (1988): 42-72.

Klein, Susan S. Handbook for achieving sex equity through education. The Johns Hopkins University Press, 701 West 40th Street, Suite 275, Baltimore, MD 21211, 1985.

Kousser, J. Morgan. "Plessy v. Ferguson." Dictionary of American History 6 (2003): 370-371.

Kumar, Deepa. "Race, ideology, and empire." Dialectical Anthropology 39, no. 1 (2015): 121.

Kymlicka, Will. "Neoliberal multiculturalism." Social resilience in the neoliberal era (2013): 99-125.

Labaree, David F. "Public goods, private goods: The American struggle over educational goals." American Educational Research Journal 34, no. 1 (1997): 39-81.

Ladson-Billings, Gloria. "Just what is critical race theory and what's it doing in a nice field like education?." International journal of qualitative studies in education 11, no. 1 (1998): 7-24.

Leake, David, and James Skouge. "Introduction to the special issue:"Self-determination" as a social construct: Cross-cultural considerations." Review of Disability Studies: An International Journal 8, no. 1 (2014).

Leary, Mark R., and June Price Tangney, eds. Handbook of self and identity. Guilford Press, 2011.

Leavitt, Peter A., Rebecca Covarrubias, Yvonne A. Perez, and Stephanie A. Fryberg. ""Frozen in Time": The Impact of Native American Media Representations on Identity and Self-Understanding." Journal of Social Issues 71, no. 1 (2015): 39-53.

Lee, Cynthia. "Making race salient: Trayvon Martin and implicit bias in a not yet post-racial society." (2013).

Lee, Stacy J. Unraveling the" model minority" stereotype: Listening to Asian American youth. Teachers College Press, 2015.

Lemke, Thomas, Monica J. Casper, and Lisa Jean Moore. Biopolitics: An advanced introduction. NYU Press, 2011.

Leonard, Geoffrey, and Laura Misumi. "WAIT (Why Am I Talking?): A Dialogue on Solidarity,

Allyship, and Supporting the Struggle for Racial Justice without Reproducing White Supremacy." Harvard Journal of African American Public Policy (2016): 61.

Lerner, Harriet E. "Early origins of envy and devaluation of women: Implications for sex role stereotypes." Bulletin of the Menninger Clinic 38, no. 6 (1974): 538.

Lind, Amy. ""Out" in International Relations: Why Queer Visibility Matters." International Studies Review 16, no. 4 (2014): 601-604.

Linder, Chris, and Katrina L. Rodriguez. "Learning from the experiences of self-identified women of color activists." Journal of College Student Development 53, no. 3 (2012): 383-398.

Lipsitz, George. "The possessive investment in whiteness: Racialized social democracy and the" white" problem in American studies." American Quarterly 47, no. 3 (1995): 369-387.

Lipsitz, George. The possessive investment in whiteness: How white people profit from identity politics. Temple University Press, 2006.

López, Ian Haney. Dog whistle politics: How coded racial appeals have reinvented racism and wrecked the middle class. Oxford University Press, 2015.

Lorde, Audre. "The master's tools will never dismantle the master's house." Feminist postcolonial theory: A reader 25 (2003): 27.

Lowe, Lisa. Immigrant acts: on Asian American cultural politics. Duke University Press, 1996.

Lubitow, Amy, and Mia Davis. "Pastel injustice: The corporate use of pinkwashing for profit." Environmental Justice 4, no. 2 (2011): 139-144.

Lugg, Catherine A. "Sissies, faggots, lezzies, and dykes: Gender, sexual orientation, and a new politics of education?." Educational Administration Quarterly 39, no. 1 (2003): 95-134.

Luibhéid, Eithne, and Lionel Cantú Jr. Queer migrations: Sexuality, US citizenship, and border crossings. U of Minnesota Press, 2005.

Lutz, Catherine. "Making war at home in the United States: Militarization and the current crisis." American Anthropologist 104, no. 3 (2002): 723-735.

Macias, Reynaldo F. "Inheriting sins while seeking absolution: Language diversity and national statistical data sets." DOCUMENT RESUME (1994): 23.

MacMullan, Terrance. "Facing up to Ignorance and Privilege: Philosophy of Whiteness as Public Intellectualism." Philosophy Compass 10, no. 9 (2015): 646-660.

Madigan, Tim. The burning: Massacre, destruction, and the Tulsa Race Riot of 1921. Macmillan, 2001.

Mahoney, Martha R. "Victimization or oppression? Women's lives, violence, and agency." The public nature of private violence: The discovery of domestic abuse (1994): 59-92.

Martin, Jane Roland. Educational metamorphoses: Philosophical reflections on identity and culture.p.6. Rowman & Littlefield, 2007.

Martin, Jane Roland. Educational metamorphoses: Philosophical reflections on identity and culture. Rowman & Littlefield, 2007.

Mason, Abra S. "Shelby County v. Holder: A Critical Analysis of the Post-Racial Movement's Relationship to Bystander Denial and Its Effect on Perceptions of Ongoing

Discrimination in Voting." Berkeley J. Afr.-Am. L.&Pol'y 17 (2015): i.

Matheis, Christian. "US American Border Crossings: Immigrants, Poverty and Suzanne Pharr's' Myth of Scarcity'." Philosophy in the Contemporary World 18, no. 2 (2011): 47-59.

McAdam, Doug. "Culture and social movements." In Culture and Politics, pp. 253-268. Palgrave Macmillan US, 2000.

McCall, Leslie. "The complexity of intersectionality." Signs: Journal of women in culture and society 30, no. 3 (2005): 1771-1800.

McGee, Ebony O., and David Stovall. "Reimagining Critical Race Theory in Education: Mental Health, Healing, and the Pathway to Liberatory Praxis." Educational Theory 65, no. 5 (2015): 491-511.

McGee, Ebony O., and David Stovall. "Reimagining Critical Race Theory in Education: Mental Health, Healing, and the Pathway to Liberatory Praxis." Educational Theory 65, no. 5 (2015): 491-511.

McNeil, Linda. Contradictions of school reform: Educational costs of standardized testing. Routledge, 2002.

Medina, José. The epistemology of resistance: Gender and racial oppression, epistemic injustice, and the social imagination. Oxford University Press, 2012.

Merryfield, Merry M. "Why aren't teachers being prepared to teach for diversity, equity, and global interconnectedness? A study of lived experiences in the making of multicultural and global educators." Teaching and teacher education 16, no. 4 (2000): 429-443.

Messerli, Jonathan. Horace Mann: A Biography. Knopf Books for Young Readers, 1972.

Miller, Toby. Cultural citizenship: Cosmopolitanism, consumerism, and television in a neoliberal age. Temple University Press, 2007.

Miserandino, Christine. "The spoon theory." Retrieved December 25 (2010): 2013.

Mitchell, Don. "The liberalization of free speech: Or, how protest in public space is silenced." Spaces of Contention: Spatialities and Social Movements (2016): 47.

Mitchell, Ojmarrh, Joshua C. Cochran, Daniel P. Mears, and William D. Bales. "Examining Prison Effects on Recidivism: A Regression Discontinuity Approach." Justice Quarterly (2016): 1-26.

Mogul, Joey L., Andrea J. Ritchie, and Kay Whitlock. Queer (in) justice: The criminalization of LGBT people in the United States. Vol. 5. Beacon Press, 2011

Mogul, Joey L., Andrea J. Ritchie, and Kay Whitlock. Queer (in) justice: The criminalization of LGBT people in the United States. Vol. 5. Beacon Press, 2011.

Mohanty, Chandra Talpade. "Under Western eyes: Feminist scholarship and colonial discourses." Feminist review 30 (1988): 61-88.

Montoya, Margaret E. "A brief history of Chicana/o school segregation: One rationale for affirmative action." Berkeley La Raza LJ 12 (2000): 159.

Moore, Kelly. "Political protest and institutional change: The anti-Vietnam War movement and American science." How social movements matter (1999): 97-118.

Morgenthau, Hans, and Politics Among Nations. "The struggle for power and peace." Nova York, Alfred Kopf (1948).

Mueller, John, and Karl Mueller. "Sanctions of mass destruction." Foreign Affairs (1999): 43-53.

Mullen, Harryette. "Optic white: blackness and the production of whiteness." diacritics 24, no. 2/3 (1994): 71-89.

Neblo, Michael A. "Three-fifths a racist: A typology for analyzing public opinion about race." Political Behavior 31, no. 1 (2009): 31-51.

Ng, Wendy. "Japanese American Internment." The Wiley Blackwell Encyclopedia of Race, Ethnicity, and Nationalism (2016).

Ngai, Mae M. "The architecture of race in American immigration law: A reexamination of the Immigration Act of 1924." The Journal of American History 86, no. 1 (1999): 67-92.

Nicholls, Walter. The DREAMers: How the undocumented youth movement transformed the immigrant rights debate. Stanford University Press, 2013.

Nier III, Charles L. "Perpetuation of Segregation: Toward a New Historical and Legal Interpretation of Redlining Under the Fair Housing Act." J. Marshall L. Rev. 32 (1998): 617.

Ninkovich, Frank. "The United States and Imperialism." A Companion to American Foreign Relations (2001): 79.

Nkrumah, Kwame. "Neo-Colonialism: The Last Stage of Imperialism. 1965." New York: International (1966).

Noltemeyer, Amity L., J. U. L. I. E. Mujic, and Caven S. Mcloughlin. "The history of inequity in education." Disproportionality in education: A guide to creating more equitable learning environments (2012):4.

Ohline, Howard A. "Republicanism and slavery: origins of the three-fifths clause in the United States Constitution." The William and Mary Quarterly: A Magazine of Early American History (1971): 563-584.

Olssen, Mark, and Michael A. Peters. "Neoliberalism, higher education and the knowledge economy: From the free market to knowledge capitalism." Journal of education policy 20, no. 3 (2005): 313-345.

Omi, Michael, and Howard Winant. Racial formation in the United States. Routledge, 2014.

Oswin, Natalie. "Critical geographies and the uses of sexuality: deconstructing queer space." Progress in Human Geography 32, no. 1 (2008): 89-103.

Palen, J. John, and Bruce London, eds. Gentrification, displacement, and neighborhood revitalization. SUNY Press, 1984.

Palen, J. John, and Bruce London, eds. Gentrification, displacement, and neighborhood revitalization. SUNY Press, 1984.

Parker, Alison Marie. Purifying America: Women, cultural reform, and pro-censorship activism, 1873-1933. University of Illinois Press, 1997.

Parry, Benita. "Problems in current theories of colonial discourse." Oxford Literary Review 9, no. 1 (1987): 27-58.

Pease, Donald E. Cultures of United States Imperialism. Duke University Press, 1993.

Pels, Peter. "The anthropology of colonialism: culture, history, and the emergence of western governmentality." Annual Review of Anthropology (1997): 163-183.

Perry, M. LaVora. A History of the Civil Rights Movement. Simon and Schuster, 2014.

Pommersheim, Frank. Broken Landscape: Indians, Indian Tribes, and the Constitution. Oxford University Press, 2009.

Power, Samantha. "A problem from hell": America and the age of genocide. Basic Books, 2013.

Quadagno, Jill S. The color of welfare: How racism undermined the war on poverty. Oxford University Press, 1994.

Quinn, Thomas C., and Julie Overbaugh. "HIV/AIDS in women: an expanding epidemic." Science 308, no. 5728 (2005): 1582-1583.

Reiman, Jeffrey, and Paul Leighton. The rich get richer and the poor get prison: Ideology, class, and criminal justice. Routledge, 2015.

Reimers, Cordelia W. "Labor market discrimination against Hispanic and black men." The review of economics and statistics (1983): 570-579

Richardson, Matt. The Queer Limit of Black Memory: Black Lesbian Literature and Irresolution. Columbus: Ohio State University Press, 2013.

Ridgeway, Cecilia L., and Shelley J. Correll. "Unpacking the gender system a theoretical perspective on gender beliefs and social relations." Gender & society 18, no. 4 (2004): 510-531.

Roberts, Dorothy. Killing the black body: Race, reproduction, and the meaning of liberty. Vintage, 2014.

Rodriguez, N. "Emptying the content of whiteness." White reign: Deploying whiteness in America (1998): 31-62.

Rose, Mike. Why school?: Reclaiming education for all of us. New Press, The, 2014.

Rothenberg, Paula S. Race, class, and gender in the United States: An integrated study. Macmillan, 2004.

Rouse, Roger. "Mexican migration and the social space of postmodernism." Diaspora: a journal of transnational Studies 1, no. 1 (1991): 8-23.

Saeed, Amir. "Media, racism and Islamophobia: The representation of Islam and Muslims in the media." Sociology Compass 1, no. 2 (2007): 443-462.

Saito, Natsu Taylor. "Whose Liberty-Whose Security-The USA PATRIOT Act in the Context of COINTELPRO and the Unlawful Repression of Political Dissent." Or. L. Rev. 81 (2002): 1051.

Schlozman, Kay Lehman, Sidney Verba, and Henry E. Brady. The unheavenly chorus: Unequal political voice and the broken promise of American democracy. Princeton University Press, 2012.

Schrecker, Ellen. The lost soul of higher education: Corporatization, the assault on academic freedom, and the end of the American university. The New Press, 2010.

Shapiro, Sidney A. "Political Oversight and the Deterioration of Regulatory Policy." Administrative Law Review (1994): 1-40.

Shohat, Ella, and Robert Stam. Unthinking Eurocentrism: Multiculturalism and the media. Routledge, 2014.

Siegel, Reva B. "Constitutional Culture, Social Movement Conflict and Constitutional Change: The Case of the De Facto Era. 2005-06 Brennan Center Symposium Lecture." California law review 94, no. 5 (2006): 1323-1419.

Simon, Herbert A. "Bounded rationality." In Utility and probability, pp. 15-18. Palgrave Macmillan UK, 1990.

Simpson, George Eaton, and J. Milton Yinger. Racial and cultural minorities: An analysis of prejudice and discrimination. Springer Science & Business Media, 2013.

Singer, Joseph William. "Canons of Conquest: The Supreme Court's Attack on Tribal Sovereignty." New Eng. L. Rev. 37 (2002): 641.

Singh, Jaideep. "A New American Apartheid: Racialized, religious minorities in the post-9/11 era." Sikh Formations 9, no. 2 (2013): 115-144.

Skocpol, Theda, Peter Evans, and Dietrich Rueschemeyer. "Bringing the state back in." Cambridge (1999).

Slater, Tom. "Looking at the" North American city" through the lens of gentrification discourse." Urban Geography 23, no. 2 (2002): 131-153.

Slaughter, Anne-Marie. "Disaggregated sovereignty: Towards the public accountability of global government net-works." Government and Opposition 39, no. 2 (2004): 159-190.

Sleeter, Christine E. "How white teachers construct race." The RoutledgeFalmer reader in multicultural education (2004): 163-178.

Smith, Andrea. "Indigeneity, settler colonialism, white suprema-cy." Racial formation in the twenty-first century (2012): 66-90.

Smith, Carly Parnitzke, and Jennifer J. Freyd. "Institutional betray-al." American Psychologist 69, no. 6 (2014): 575.

Smith, Karen E., and Margot Light. Ethics and foreign policy. Cambridge University Press, 2001.

Smith, Valerie. Not just race, not just gender: Black feminist readings. Routledge, 2013.

Smith, William A. "Black faculty coping with racial battle fatigue: The campus racial climate in a post-civil rights era." A long way to go: Conversations about race by African American faculty and graduate students 14 (2004).

Smitherman, Geneva. ""What Is Africa to Me?": Language, Ideolo-gy, and African American." American Speech 66, no. 2 (1991): 115-132.

Snyderman, Mark, and R. J. Herrnstein. "Intelligence tests and the Immigration Act of 1924." American Psychologist 38, no. 9 (1983): 986.

Solomon, Barbara Miller. In the company of educated women: A history of women and higher education in America. Yale University Press, 1985.

Solorzano, Daniel G., and Octavio Villalpando. "Critical race theory, marginality, and the experience of students of color in higher education." Sociology of education: Emerging perspec-tives (1998): 21.

Spohn, Cassia. "Racial disparities in prosecution, sentencing, and punishment." The Oxford handbook of ethnicity, crime, and immigration (2013): 166-193.

Spring, Joel. Deculturalization and the struggle for equality: A brief history of the education of dominated cultures in the United States. Routledge, 2016.

Stark, Evan. "Coercive control." Violence against women: Current theory and practice in domestic abuse, sexual violence and exploitation (2013): 17-33.

Steele, Shelby. "White guilt." The American Scholar 59, no. 4 (1990): 497-506.

Steuter, Erin, and Deborah Wills. At war with metaphor: media, propaganda, and racism in the war on terror. Lexington Books, 2009.

Stolzenberg, Nomi Maya. "" He Drew a Circle That Shut Me out": Assimilation, Indoctrination, and the Paradox of a Liberal Education." Harvard Law Review (1993): 581-667.

Stoskopf, Alan. "Echoes of a forgotten past: Eugenics, testing, and education reform." In The Educational Forum, vol. 66, no. 2, pp. 126-133. Taylor & Francis Group, 2002.

Sudbury, Julia. Global lockdown: Race, gender, and the prison-industrial complex. Routledge, 2014.

Sugarman, Stephen D., and Ellen G. Widess. "Equal protection for non-English-speaking school children: Lau v. Nichols." California Law Review 62, no. 1 (1974): 157-182.

Sullivan, Shannon. The Physiology of Sexist and Racist Oppression. Oxford University Press, 2015.

Tascón, Sonia, and Jim Ife. "Human Rights and Critical Whiteness: Whose Humanity?." International Journal of Human Rights 12, no. 3 (2008): 307-327.

Taubman, Peter Maas. Teaching by numbers: Deconstructing the discourse of standards and accountability in education. Routledge, 2010.

Theoharis, George. "Social justice educational leaders and resistance: Toward a theory of social justice leadership." Educational administration quarterly 43, no. 2 (2007): 221-258.

Ticktin, Miriam. "Sexual violence as the language of border control: where French feminist and anti-immigrant rhetoric meet." Signs: Journal of Women in Culture and Society 33, no. 4 (2008): 863-889.

Tirman, John. "Immigration and insecurity: post-9/11 fear in the United States." MIT Center for International Studies Audit of the Conventional Wisdom (2006): 06-09.

Tjaden, Patricia, and Nancy Thoennes. "Prevalence, Incidence, and Consequences of Violence against Women: Findings from the National Violence against Women Survey. Research in Brief." (1998).

Tomlinson, Sally. A sociology of special education (RLE Edu M). Routledge, 2012.

Turnbull, Ann P. Exceptional lives: Special education in today's schools. Merrill/Prentice Hall, Order Department, 200 Old Tappan Rd., Old Tappan, NJ 07675., 1995.

Tyack, David B. The one best system: A history of American urban education. Vol. 95, pp.180. Harvard University Press, 1974.

Ussher, Jane M. "Diagnosing difficult women and pathologising femininity: Gender bias in psychiatric nosology." Feminism & Psychology 23, no. 1 (2013): 63-69.

Valdes, Francisco. "Unpacking hetero-patriarchy: tracing the conflation of sex, gender & (and) sexual orientation to its origins." Yale JL & Human. 8 (1996): 161.

Van Dijk, Teun A. "Discourse, power and access." Texts and practices: Readings in critical discourse analysis (1996): 84-104.

Walker, Renee E., Christopher R. Keane, and Jessica G. Burke. "Disparities and access to healthy food in the United States: A review of food deserts literature." Health & place 16, no. 5 (2010): 876-884.

Ware, Norma C., Kim Hopper, Toni Tugenberg, Barbara Dickey, and Daniel Fisher. "Connectedness and citizenship: Redefining social integration." Psychiatric Services 58, no. 4 (2007): 469-474.

Waterstone, Michael. "Untold Story of the Rest of the Americans with Disabilities Act, The." Vand. L. Rev. 58 (2005): 1807.

Waymer, Damion, and Robert L. Heath. "Black Voter Dilution, American Exceptionalism, and Racial Gerrymandering The Paradox of the Positive in Political Public Relations." Journal of Black Studies (2016): 0021934716649646.

Webb, Maureen. Illusions of security: Global surveillance and democracy in the post-9/11 world. City Lights Books, 2007.

Weintraub, Frederick J., Alan Abeson, and Jeffrey Zettel. "The End of Quiet Revolution: The Education for All Handicapped Children Act of 1975." Exceptional Children 44, no. 2 (1977): 114-128.

Wexler, Lisa Marin, Gloria DiFluvio, and Tracey K. Burke. "Resilience and marginalized youth: Making a case for personal and collective meaning-making as part of resilience research in public health." Social science & medicine 69, no. 4 (2009): 565-570.

Wilson II, Clint C., Felix Gutierrez, and Lena Chao. Racism, sexism, and the media: The rise of class communication in multicultural America. Sage, 2003.

Woods, Jeff R. Black Struggle, Red Scare: Segregation and Anti-Communism in the South, 1948--1968. LSU Press, 2003.

Woodward, Comer Vann. The strange career of Jim Crow. Oxford University Press, USA, 1955.

Yell, Mitchell L. The law and special education. Merrill/Prentice-Hall, Inc., 200 Old Tappan Road, Old Tappan, NJ 07675, 1998.

Yinger, John. Closed doors, opportunities lost: The continuing costs of housing discrimination. Russell Sage Foundation, 1995.

Young, James O., and Conrad G. Brunk. The ethics of cultural appropriation. John Wiley & Sons, 2012.

Young, Robert. White mythologies: Writing history and the West. Psychology Press, 2004.

Yuval-Davis, Nira. "Dialogical epistemology—an intersectional resistance to the "oppression Olympics"." Gender & society 26, no. 1 (2012): 46-54.

Zemsky, Beth, and Ronni L. Sanlo. "Do policies matter?." New Directions for Student Services 2005, no. 111 (2005): 7-15.

Ziltener, Patrick, and Daniel Künzler. "Impacts of Colonialism-A Research Survey." Journal of World-Systems Research 19, no. 2 (2013): 290.

Zoysa, Richard de. "America's foreign policy: Manifest Destiny or Great Satan?." Contemporary Politics 11, no. 2-3 (2005): 133-156.

Index

www.ingramcontent.com/pod-product-compliance
Lightning Source LLC
Chambersburg PA
CBHW072131020426
42334CB00018B/1758